THE FORCING HOUSE

OR

THE COCKPIT CONTINUED

Tragi-Comedy in Four Acts

BY

ISRAEL ZANGWILL

New York
THE MACMILLAN COMPANY
1923

180446

TO MAURICE MAETERLINCK

MY DEAR MAETERLINCK,—

The coincidence that this play was written in your neighbourhood, and that "The Cockpit" of which it is the sequel was dedicated to your first translator, our common friend, Sutro, suggests my inscribing it to the memory of the holiday month you and I spent together twenty years ago, tramping the delectable regions you have since chosen for your dwelling-place. In those sunlit winter walks, eternalised in your exquisite essay on "The Sources of Spring," a frequent theme of our discussions was the nature of Time. You in those days favoured a fixed Eternity in which the future already existed as much as the past, so that one could imagine going backwards or forwards in it: a conception since illustrated by the cinematograph. I on the other hand was all for the essential reality of Time, with an insistence that would now be called Bergsonian, and I would have none of the fatalism involved in your conception. A tramway-collision, immediately after one of these discussions, left me injured and you unhurt but the argument anent Fate unimpaired on either side. I could wish, however, that you had been in the right and that it were possible to go back in Time, to tread over again those rocky olive-green by-ways and track together the sources of our springtide.

v

The nature of the Drama was not, so far as I remember, ever debated with my fellow-Peripatetic. Possibly I acquiesced in the profound preface you had contributed to friend Sutro's first published play, "The Cave of Illusion," in which you lamented that the decay of supernatural beliefs had robbed the dramatist of that background of depth, mystery and grandeur against which the figures of the classic tragedies had been set. Possibly I sympathised with the demand in your essay on *Le Tragique Quotidien* for a Drama of the Future, which should be almost a still-life drama: inasmuch as for us cultured moderns crude external violence had almost vanished from the planet, so that "we who lived far from blood and cries and swords," whose "tears had become silent, invisible, almost spiritual," felt on visiting a theatre, as if we were "passing some hours with our ancestors." The Sage sitting by his lamp, a hand opening or closing a door, a ray of light through a casement, a shadow on a blind, these, you urged, were the only legitimate effects open to the modern dramatist, if his colour-scale was to be as subdued and subtle as life's. Assuredly your own contributions to this quietist theatre—immortal creations like "L'Intruse" or "Intérieur"—had not disposed me to question its programme—would indeed you could "recapture that first fine careless rapture!" They may even have disposed me to accept the optimism of your subsequent essay on *Le Drame Moderne,* in which, anticipating a clarification of the human conscience and a broadening of human love, you looked forward to a theatre whence not only

vi

external violence but even ugly internal passions should be banished, "a theatre of peace, of beauty without tears." Perhaps if I left that phase of serene faith unquestioned, it was because of your impatience with the scepticism of the race of Ecclesiastes. And yet it was the Pagan poet of an imperial people who saw that tears are not to be banished, that the texture of life, even at its peacefullest, is irretrievably tragic: *sunt lachrymae rerum.*

Ten years after you had penned this dream of "a theatre without tears," your country was invaded. You had said that "violated virgins and imprisoned citizens" were but the outworn motifs of the obsolescent theatre of "blood, external tears and death." Alas, you now saw all Belgium as a violated virgin, your own tears fell over "ruins and sacrifices, nameless tortures and numberless dead," and in your philippic, "The Hour of Destiny," the whilom Pacifist philosopher urged revenge and destruction "root and branch," "even against our own sense of pity and generosity." I did not need your assurance to me that you had modified your view of the scope and function of the modern stage. Your play, "The Burgomaster of Stilemonde," was your own most eloquent comment on your early conception, if indeed "Monna Vanna" had not anticipated its awakening to the "external" world.

But what you had felt constructively as a poet, lesser souls had been feeling in their negative prosaic fashion. In an essay on "The War and the Drama," I pointed out that among our dramatic critics—drawn for the most part from the genteel circles of a sophisticated and pacific civilisation—a similar reaction against violence had taken place, if without the Maeterlinckian profundity. They had seen the drama become —in the Robertsonian theatre—a storm in a teacup. They had seen the disappearance of the robustious actor and the growth of the natural, if not always audible, *jeune premier*. They believed—with that admirable light comedian, Sir Charles Hawtrey—that the day of the high tragedian was over, though he might linger on in those occasional galvanizations of Shakespeare which piety for the dead classics would continue to inspire. But, in truth, Shakespeare seemed as barbarous to them as he had seemed to Voltaire. In their ignorance of life, all the flamboyance of passion and colour, all the odd gleams of purity and beauty, all the pathos and grotesquerie that challenge the artist's eye from Clapham to Martaban, had ceased to exist for them when those things went out of fashion on the stage. All characters not common as city clerks were improbable; sentiments not expressed currently in drawing-rooms were fustian. They recognised comedy by soda-water syphons and cigarettes, and melodrama by pistols. That pistols might consist with comedy, or cigarettes with tragedy—even blank verse tragedy —they could not conceive.

But it was not a dramatic critic, it was a thinker— and no lesser thinker than George Santayana—who as late as 1913 complained, if not quite in the schoolboyish spirit of Stevenson and Henley yearning for bloodshed, that "the hue of daily adventure is dull . . . our bodies in this generation are generally safe and comfortable . . . the whole drift of things presents a huge good-natured comedy to the observer."

Personally I was saved by my daily business of plucking Jews out of the pale of Christian massacre from regarding modern life as altogether "a huge good-natured comedy." That generous spirit, Octave Mirbeau, who had hailed you as "The Belgian Shakespeare," gave in one of his books so heartrending an account of a pogrom in Russian Jewry, taken from the life—or should one say, the death?—that no Parisian critic had any excuse for thinking that the spectacle he beheld from his club window exhausted the contingencies of contemporary existence. There was in fact even before the war so much mass-tragedy in being —one need only mention the Congo or Armenian atrocities—that it should not have needed the explosion of Europe to confound Mr. Santayana's "observer." It should not have needed famine and pestilence, poison-gas and flame-propellers, cannibalism and the return of the wolf, the murder or exile of Emperors, the overthrow of dynasties and economic systems, to remind him over what a thin volcanic crust our "huge good-natured comedy" went a-tripping.

Yet even after all these experiences, so accustomed had our urban civilisation become to its drab surface and its shallow security, so set is the human mind, in which prepossession is nine points of the law, that despite the monstrous happenings in Ireland at this very moment, a drama holding up the mirror to natural phenomena of this order is still liable to be classed as "melodramatic." The word was recently applied by a critic to a revival of an old play of mine that had come straight out of the heart of my work for Jewish emigrants.

Not that my critic understood that "melodrama" taken literally is the art of Æschylus or Sophocles. He used the word in that debased sense which it had acquired in our popular theatres, wherein strong situations are dissociated from psychology or probability, and life is distorted by sentimentality, and destiny moves—in a reversed Hellenic direction—to a happy matrimonial ending. These transpontine theatres had become the sole purveyors of the drama of violence, to them all strong situations had been surrendered, and their presentation of incidents cut off from character had led to the notion that what constituted melodrama was its situations. But if theatrical situations rooted in psychology be melodramatic, then those plays of Racine which the Comédie Française interprets with such impressive art, would have to come under the contemned label. There is an excellent word "dramatic" which seems to have gone quite out of fashion. It should surely be revived, for it covers ground otherwise undefined. The name of Sardou—that master of dramatic technique—is rarely mentioned nowadays without a sneer. I used to speak of him myself as a stage-carpenter. But closer acquaintance with his plays and especially with his prefaces has convinced me that, although he may have sometimes divorced incidents from their roots in psychology, he was as frequently dramatic in the best sense, and that his starting-point was not so much *une scène à faire* as a moral idea. His play with the unfortunately melodramatic title of *L'Affaire des Poisons,* contains one of the noblest characters and some of the finest scenes known to me in all drama. In conceiving the drama as primarily dramatic, Sardou was superbly right. The drama should be dramatic, just as the stage should be stagy. The obloquy attaching to staginess was originally aimed at its transference from the stage to real life. As dirt is matter in the wrong place, so staginess is manner in the wrong place. It is by a curious retroversion that censure is associated with staginess even in the right place. There was finality in the dictum of Goethe that we call Art Art because it is not Nature.

The fact that the drama is meant to be acted, places it in a specific category of Art, differentiates it from all other forms of literature, and removes it irrevocably from realism in any narrow sense. It must weave at once with a double thread a play as well as a story. Confined to a few feet of space, and a few hours of time, it must achieve a concentration and a tenseness undemanded of the novelist. Though the tension may be relaxed in comedy, in serious work a slackening is fatal. But to be serious about trifles is absurd, so that if strong passions and situations are withdrawn from the legitimate area of the dramatist's art, the drama proper must inevitably perish, and the comedian reign sole, *"vacuâ in aulâ."*

So far, however, from such narrowing of the drama's scope being necessitated by the nature of our epoch, it is melodrama, almost in its popular signification, that the war has vindicated. Life, I sum up the lesson, is still heroic and vulgar in the grandiose old fashion. There are soldiers, not chocolate but iron, there are traitors and bullies. There are clamorous and riotous crowds that pillage and run amok, there are lovemakings and clownings under the shadow of death, there are monstrous coincidences, impudently improbable. Even the spy does, it appears, really exist.

Nevertheless Heraclitus was right, and the same river never runs twice into the sea. The drama, if it is to go on holding "the mirror up to nature," must show the age its particular "form and pressure." It is clear that the author who assigned this function to the drama would not have been writing Shakespearean plays, had he lived to-day. The occasional exploitation of "the divine William" is less a sign of grace than of the dearth of a living poetic drama, and our stage, in which he alone represents high art, makes on me the effect which I have elsewhere compared to that of a savage dressed exclusively in a top hat. The safe and obvious resource of managements or actors aiming at classic rank or the reputation of culture, Shakespeare but serves to bar out still more effectually any attempt to replace or supplement his artistic convention, or to express, if I may misapply Whitman:

"Years of the modern, years of the unperformed."

As the Bible has become the enemy of religion, so is Shakespeare the enemy of the British drama.

How far the blame for the absence of a modern heroic drama is to be divided among dramatists, man-

xii

agers, critics and the public is a complex question. That the fault lies more with the managers than with the public may be seen from the steady success of high art at such a People's Theatre as the Old Vic. But the dramatists have also their share of responsibility. There is indeed, as Santayana complained in 1913, a decay of seriousness in all the arts which are—"like truant children who think their life will be glorious if they only run away and play for ever; no need is felt of a dominant ideal passion and theme, nor of any moral interest in the interpretation of nature." One can imagine that the war would not have lessened Santayana's sense of the need of an art not all play. It set M. Victor Giraud, the editor of the *Revue des Deux Mondes,* expressing this very demand for a "dominant ideal passion and theme," as well as a "moral interest." He echoed too your old cry for a modern framework. The war, he urged, with its great moral issues and its high fate-driven personages had provided the themes, it but remained for the modern dramatist to find the framework. With all respect, it seems to me that a modern picture is infinitely more important than a modern frame. Your new "internal" theatre may have needed a new framework and you found a beautiful one, but seeing that the old "external" theatre of violence must persist in the mirror of art, is it really necessary to look "behind the looking-glass"? Our Thomas Hardy invented for his epical drama of "The Dynasts" a new machinery of Spirits of Irony and Pity. But for all the conviction they carry, he might as well have reanimated the archangels of Milton. "Life itself," as I urged in the essay already cited, "offers every element of pathos and mystery, of horror and devilry, that poetic dignity demands. Out of the clash and conflict of the forces of life the modern dramatist may build a tragedy as noble and unadorned as a Doric temple rising 'twixt sea and sky on its rocky headland."

This present play makes, of course, no pretence to be that tragedy. It even labels itself a tragi-comedy. Its order of architecture is Corinthian, not Doric, for it is difficult to handle in simple tragic outline a theme so complex, so bristling with contemporary questions and problems. The theme is at any rate immune from the danger of critical ignorance of its existence. "Bolshevism" indeed has become an obsession; it is one of those words which people put into their mouths to steal away their brains. That is why I have tabooed the word in my play. Socialism or Communism had been in the air all my lifetime and long before I was born. An infinity of treatises, novels, journals, plays and speeches in every language under the sun had dealt with it. I myself had weighed its pros and cons twelve years ago in my "Italian Fantasies." "We are all Socialists now," said that distinguished English statesman, Sir William Harcourt, who was already dead a decade before the war. Yet to-day Socialism sets the mouth of the world agape with horror as at some dread diabolical novelty fallen suddenly from the blue. Only less comic than this consternation of "the bourgeois" is the dismay of the Socialists, their haste to disavow their progeny.

For my own part, nothing that has happened has contradicted my published prevision of the course Socialism would run, and my handling of the theme dramatically would have been substantially the same had Russia been as imaginary a country as my Valdania, though I have, of course, profited by the Russian experience to add a concrete touch or two. There is, equally of course, no attempt to photograph facts and personages. The artist needs free elbow-room and must profit by his "poetic license." As Renan pointed out in the preface to his own play, *Le Prêtre de Nemi,* by the side of real history there is also ideal history which has not occurred literally, and yet is essentially a summary of historic realities. No less apposite is his remark in the same preface that it should be impossible to refute a thorough work of art, for "the other side of every thought ought to be indicated in it, so that the reader may seize at one glance the two opposite sides of which the truth is composed." The Jewish psychology of Trotsky offered a rich and tempting model, but it would have over-weighted the theme and I set him aside for a simpler type of leader. Moreover Russia is not the only country where the dread "new" disease has raged. The pioneer country seems to have been Mexico, and you may be interested to hear that the young man who took a snapshot of you, when you lunched with me at my hotel, was the son of the very President of Mexico in whose period of office "Bolshevism" broke out. Naturally he supplied me with vivid details of the movement that had ruined his family and made of him a precocious Conservative.

My Prologue is already too long, but looking over what I have written, I find a certain farcical futility in writing on the philosophic aspects of the theatre, when the main factor of that institution is economic. In a country where, despite Matthew Arnold, the theatre remains unorganised, where there is no care for art nor curiosity about life, can one erect a noble contemporary drama upon a paying basis? How far those cynics are right who reduce all history, however high-flown, to economics I will not pretend to determine. But the economic basis of drama is unfortunately beyond question.

> "The drama's laws the drama's patrons give,
> And they who live to please must please to live."

The Utilitarian Philosophy had a formula which might almost have been invented to express the secret of dramatic success. The play must produce "the greatest happiness of the greatest number." It must express, therefore, the lowest common measure of culture, the most normal emotion and vision. Mr. Bernard Shaw, in his preface to one of his plays, calculates at seventy or a hundred thousand the number of patrons who must indirectly put their money together to enable a play to run. But in these days, when to score your century on the stage no longer demonstrates success but merely the avoidance of failure, a hundred thousand spectators will not carry you very long. And Mr. Shaw has omitted the most important item in the calculation. For "the first hundred thousand" must precipitate themselves in the first hundred

xvi

days, nay, the signs of the rush must appear from the moment of production. "Delays are dangerous," says Bacon. But in the theatre they are fatal. That leisurely respite during which the book may educate taste, win appreciation and gather momentum is impossible in a theatre, where at least a hundred pounds are oozing away every evening. Thus the herd mind must not only find itself mirrored in the play, it must discover this at once and be drawn theatrewards, "as the deer breaks, as the steer breaks."

Hitherto London managements have been prepared to accept moderate houses all the week, provided they could rely on "bumper houses" at the two Saturday performances. But it now appears from an interview with a manager that, by reason of the rising prices, a play will have to be withdrawn, unless at every performance it can "play to capacity." The gravity of this situation is obvious. It lowers still further the quality by extending the quantity of spectators necessary to make ends meet. And if relief is sought in higher prices, the public may be still more driven to the cinema, with his smaller demand on the pocket as on the brain. Between this Scylla and Charybdis the finer forms of drama must surely suffer shipwreck .

Shakespeare said "all the world's a stage." It is a pity he spoiled the profundity of the remark by detailing the sense in which he meant it. It is in the social comedy that men and women are "merely players." (Shakespeare should have written "players" in Greek —"hypocrites" to wit.) And the players themselves, being merely men and women, are equally compelled

xvii

to the hypocrisy of life. The theatre's form of the social comedy is to run a business under the guise of an art. In his green-room slang, the actor has always called his play-house a "shop." He should now call it a gambling-house. For it is no longer run even as an industry, but persists by a perpetual change of ruined speculators, lured on by the dazzle of the few lucky punters. Save in two or three theatres, in which the presence of an actor-manager or an ambitious tyro gives a certain constancy, there is no stage in London whose fare is fixed, still less does any exist constituted to receive such pieces as "The Forcing House." In your timeless Eternity it may, for aught I know, be already in performance—even on the films—but it was assuredly not inspired by any hopes of gold or glory from the contemporary stage.

And yet it was not designed any the more for a "closet drama." But fortunately the dual nature of the drama, which can exist without actors, though the actors cannot exist without it, makes it possible for a drama written expressly for ultimate or posthumous performance, to enjoy a sufficient life in its literary embodiment—or disembodiment. Through this medium I have had almost as much pleasure from Mr. Drinkwater's "Oliver Cromwell"—a play that, I am sure will pay when some manager with boldness and brains arises—as from an actual performance. In reading French plays—those of François de Curel for example—I have enjoyed myself more than at most French theatres, and without the drawbacks of the journey, the price of a stall, or the elderly French harpies. The concentration of life, which is drama, the rapidity with which one arrives at the essence of the situation, is infinitely exhilarating after the average novel, especially to one who can read a play as a musician reads a score—and for those who cannot, it should be eked out by stage directions and descriptions, first found, I believe, in the published plays of Oscar Wilde.

The practice of publishing new plays is growing in England and contributing by reflex action to the elevation of our literary standard of drama, already improved by the accession to the theatre of almost all our men of letters (though they give it only their second-best). "I always say to dramatists, publish your play," Henry James observed to me once. "Publish your play if you are not ashamed of it. Let us see what your success looks like in cold print." The practice was indeed dismally discouraged by the Press, for, while the author was hoping to bring his work before a higher and more leisured court than the bench of dramatic criticism, he found his book almost invariably dismissed with the words: "Text of the play produced at the so-and-so Theatre." You could not even "publish and be damned." If, on the other hand, the play had not been produced, it might not be noticed at all. "The published play seems to be the Cinderella of literature," a boycotted dramatist lamented. He must have forgotten Cinderella's ultimate fate.

But even for the non-production of a play on the stage there is ample compensation. I am not thinking of the freedom from stage censorship, for the thought of the Lord Chamberlain, though he still keeps a play

xix

of mine under embargo, has never hampered my pen in the faintest. Nor have I in mind the inevitable materialisation and refraction which made Charles Lamb prefer Shakespeare unstaged, and impaired for me the charm of your own "Blue Bird." No, the compensation is physological. For while playwriting, despite all the pains of parturition, is life-enhancing, play-producing is life-destroying. Business managers were sufficiently katabolic, but no self-respecting man of letters can have truck with mere gamblers. Even contact with one's actors, delightful as they can be, and much as they may vivify one's work, is not conducive to longevity. My youthful epigram that for the actor, despite Euclid, the part is greater than the whole, has had a flattering currency. But it has not changed the player's psychology. Even such a lord of the European stage as the author of "Pygmalion"—we gather from a managerial indiscretion—has not been spared desperate combats with his leading lady. Whether under the Socialism he favours he will be able to tame his tigress, or whether he himself will find his own claws pared, is an interesting speculation, with which I ring up the curtain on this tragi-comedy of Communism.

Commending it to your gracious mercies and hoping that my association of it with your name will not tend to diminish your friendship,

I am,

Cordially yours,

ISRAEL ZANGWILL.

Midsummer, 1922.

xx

THE FORCING HOUSE

DRAMATIS PERSONÆ:

RIFFONI VITTORIO	*A Socialist*
PROFESSOR SALARET	*A Socialist Writer*
COUNT CAZOTTI	*Prime Minister of Valdania*
BARON GRIPSTEIN	*A Financier*
DUKE D'AZOLLO	*Formerly Ex-Regent of Valdania*
MARSHAL ROXO	*Ex-War Minister*
COLONEL MOLP	*Head of the Royal Body-Guard*
CORPORAL VANNI	*Of the Palace Guards*
BRIO	*Gripstein's Majordomo*
OMAR	*Gripstein's Doorkeeper*
MARGHERITA	*Queen of Valdania*
LIVIA (BARONESS SIGISMONDO GRIPSTEIN)	*Gripstein's Daughter-in-Law*
SIGNORA DA GRASSO	*Wife of a Valdanian Landowner*
COUNTESS CAZOTTI	*Wife of the Prime Minister*

Guests, Lackeys and Guards

The action passes in our day at Scaletta, the capital of Valdania.

Act I in Baroness Gripstein's salon, Acts II, III and IV in the former Throne Room of the old San Marco Palace.

(In the description of scenes, R. and L. stand for Right and Left of the actor, not the spectator, from whose point of view they can be read transposed.)

xxiv

ACT ONE

The scene is a salon in BARON GRIPSTEIN'S *house at Scaletta, the capital of Valdania, on a spring evening. The room has been made by dividing and partly modernising a vast ancient banqueting hall, the unseen portion of which, behind modern folding doors in the rear wall, constitutes the dining-room. The furniture is massive, and there are tapestries and old oil-portraits and religious pictures, but the mediæval gloom, which the electric candles in sconces cannot quite dissipate, is dispelled by the masses of hothouse roses in the great old vases. In the lower part of the left wall is a tall Gothic leaden-paned casement with a cushioned seat, opening on the courtyard. The original old doors, oaken and brass-studded, are in the centre of the right and the upper part of the left wall.* OMAR, *the Moslem doorkeeper, clad in fez and robes, is going out obsequiously* L., *when he is recalled by the magnificent majordomo,* BRIO, *who, attired in Western evening dress, is holding in his white-gloved hand a menu and a music-programme, both printed on satin.*

BRIO

Wait, Omar. I forgot to explain to you that when Her Majesty arrives, she cannot be left like the other guests to come upstairs of herself. The Baron must be already below to welcome her. And the Baroness Sigismondo, too, of course, since she is acting as hostess for her father-in-law. See that you warn them in time.

I

OMAR
But how, Signor Brio, shall I know when Her Majesty is arriving? I am not a prophet of Allah.

BRIO
A gendarme from the courtyard must apprise you.

OMAR
It is a word of wisdom. But would wisdom had inspired Colonel Molp to plant more gendarmes! Already the courtyard is invaded and the carpet and the awning are besieged by a godless crowd.

BRIO
Not so godless, Omar. Open that window and you will hear them crying out against the Jew's presumption in entertaining the Queen of Valdania.

OMAR [*Firing up*]
It is their own presumption, if you will forgive mine, Signor Brio. Since it pleases Her Majesty to honour our master. . . .

BRIO [*With a wry face*]
Our *master!* Well, well, these are hard times, Omar. But what need was there for the Queen to stoop, too? However, I see you Moslems are at heart more for the Jews than for us Christians.

OMAR
It is only Her Majesty that I have at heart, Signor Brio.
    [*The handle of the door* R. *of the men turns.*]

BRIO
Hush! To your duties.
[*As* OMAR *goes out by the door* L. BARON GRIPSTEIN
enters by the door R. *This florid but white-haired
and sympathetic personage of Semitic appearance
is dressed for dinner and wears the sash of the
Order of the Redeemer.* HE *has at this moment a
nervous, even fussy, air.*]

BARON GRIPSTEIN
The Baroness Sigismondo not down yet, Brio?

BRIO
It is much too early, Excellency.

BARON GRIPSTEIN
Not on an occasion like this. Ha! Is that the menu?

BRIO [*Giving him the satin sheets*]
This is the menu, and this the music-programme.

BARON GRIPSTEIN
Debussy, Strauss, Wagner—but there's not a single
one of the Queen's compositions!

BRIO
Baroness Sigismondo's orders, Excellency. Her
Majesty dislikes hearing her own compositions except
accidentally.

BARON GRIPSTEIN
Ah, if my daughter-in-law arranged it—!
    [*Returns programme*]
Who painted this menu?

3

BRIO
Klingermann, Excellency.

BARON GRIPSTEIN
But he's a German artist, not a Valdanian.

BRIO
There were not enough first-class native artists to go round. I consulted the Baroness. Your Excellency was so busy with the Bosnavinian Loan.

BARON GRIPSTEIN
But Klingermann is even a Jew! I shall be accused of patronising Jews! . . . Her Majesty's menu—that at least is Valdanian?

BRIO
By Delsio!
   [*Apologetically*]
But I had to pay him two thousand lire.

BARON GRIPSTEIN
Bravo!

BRIO
It is a water-colour of the Valley of the Vaar.

BARON GRIPSTEIN
In Bosnavina? But the Queen dislikes any reminder that she is Duchess of Bosnavina! She hates our having seized our neighbour's territory, and she regarded Governor Marrobio's assasination by a Bosnavinian patriot as a righteous nemesis.

4

BRIO
It is a womanly weakness one does not take seriously, Excellency.

BARON GRIPSTEIN
One takes it so seriously, Brio, that the Bosnavinian Loan was designed by Cazotti as much to pacify Her Majesty as Bosnavina. And it is wonderful how the inflow of capital is already quenching the ardour of Bosnavinian patriotism. In vain Rolmenia will now throw oil on the flame. Ah, Cazotti is a wonderful statesman. Don't you think so, Brio?

BRIO
It is wonderful how he is always Prime Minister!

BARON GRIPSTEIN
Ah, I see you do not share my enthusiasm. But opinion is free in Valdania—thanks to Cazotti again. I suspect you heard him slandered in the circles from which I took you.

BRIO
They said he began on a tub and would end on the throne.

BARON GRIPSTEIN
That sounds like the Duke D'Azollo. But his only tub was his journal, and considering it was he who set the Queen on the throne——!

BRIO
There are stories, Excellency, that he could not help himself; that so far from his having saved her from

5

her mother's fate by bringing her up in a Roman convent, the princess was really discovered by Roxo in America!

BARON GRIPSTEIN
Really, really, how the ducal circle can fabricate such myths or you swallow them——!
    [*With sudden agitation*]
Why is there no ham on the menu? I particularly said——

BRIO
There is, Excellency. With the madeira. The eleventh course before the sorbet.

BARON GRIPSTEIN
Oh, ah! I beg your pardon. But it is so unobtrusive. Ha! So you did get enough early strawberries!

BRIO
But they made me pay through the nose, those Jew monopolists——
    [*Stops and coughs confusedly.*]

BARON GRIPSTEIN
Business is business, Brio. We Valdanians are too hard on the Jews. The Queen loves strawberries and the Comptroller can't afford them yet for the royal table.

BRIO
And yet your Excellency admires Cazotti! Surely he ought to allow Her Majesty more money.
6

BARON GRIPSTEIN
Impossible with our post-war taxation. It would set all the Socialists shrieking. . . . I am glad to find *you're* not a Socialist, Brio.

BRIO
I? I would smoke them out like wasps.

BARON GRIPSTEIN
That's Marshal Roxo's recipe. But these drastic methods are incompatible with democracy.
   [*Handing back the menu*]
See that this Klingermann menu is put in *my* place. And give the Valley of the Vaar sketch not to the Queen but to Marshal Roxo. . . .
   [BRIO *bows*]
The *chef* is satisfied?

BRIO
He says that not since he created the pink luncheon for the Grand Duke of Baden the day the Kaiser——

BARON GRIPSTEIN
Ach, do not raise these melancholy memories. What shadows we are, Brio, even the greatest of us!

BRIO
I do not consider myself a shadow. And I shall yet live to see all the royal houses flourishing again.
   [*Exit by the folding doors, giving a glimpse of the dazzling dinner-table with more roses, and hovering lackeys.*]

7

BARON GRIPSTEIN
These cheery Valdanians!

> [*After an instant of musing, he looks nervously at his watch. Then the door* R. *opens and the* BARONESS SIGISMONDO, *a young Valdanian lady with a distinguished face and bearing, comes in. Her gown is simple but exquisite, and her only jewellery is a pearl necklace*]

Ah, Livia, at last!

LIVIA
At last? I am a full half hour too early! I hurried my toilette, knowing you would be ramping like a lion.

BARON GRIPSTEIN
Never mind—how could you make yourself *more* beautiful?

LIVIA
Make myself? One would think I were the Countess Cazotti.

> [*Moves to adjust the roses in a vase.*]

BARON GRIPSTEIN
Don't laugh at your old father-in-law. He's not used to making gallant speeches. But you might have worn his diamond necklace.

LIVIA
I'm wearing his pearl one.

BARON GRIPSTEIN
Pearls are at such a discount, now they can be made artificially.

8

LIVIA
I am not casting them before swine . . . Do put away
that watch—one would think you had never seen the
Queen.

BARON GRIPSTEIN
I've never seen her in my house. And how can I be
too grateful for the lead she is giving Society? Everybody will come now.

LIVIA [*Drily*]
Except the Duchess D'Azollo.

BARON GRIPSTEIN
But, *cara,* she's coming to-night!

LIVIA [*Still arranging roses*]
The Duchess enjoys providential headaches. I know
her from my maid of honour days. She has never for-
given me for marrying a Jew.

BARON GRIPSTEIN [*Agitated*]
A Jew? My Sigismondo is not a Jew! When was
Sigismondo converted to Judaism?

LIVIA
Yes, I know it's only a religion. But somehow—any-
how the Duchess considers herself better-born than the
Queen.

BARON GRIPSTEIN
But how is that possible?

9

LIVIA
Ask Sigismondo. He has all the genealogies at his
fingers' ends.

BARON GRIPSTEIN [*Suddenly covering his eyes
    and sobbing*]
Oh! Oh! Oh!

LIVIA
O my dear father! What is it?

BARON GRIPSTEIN
It is only at his fingers' ends that Sigismondo can have
anything. My poor blinded boy! And he won't even
see the Queen in our home!

LIVIA
He is very happy in his library, typing his history of
Alpastroom.

BARON GRIPSTEIN [*Hysterically*]
I wish Alpastroom had never existed—it was in trying
to emulate our mediæval hero that Sigismondo——

LIVIA
Don't father. It was during the war with Bosnavina
that I learnt to love Sigismondo. And genius like his
conquers even blindness. He knows exactly where I
have to look for a date or an episode.

BARON GRIPSTEIN
Ah, Livia, you are eyes to me as well as to him. Be-
reaved of wife and eldest-born, but for you I should

have gone down in blackness to the grave . . . *Carissima!*
   [*Embraces her.*]

LIVIA [*Disengaging herself gently*]
Don't ruffle the hostess's chevelure.
   [OMAR *enters through the door to their left and presents to the* BARON *a card on a silver salver.*]

BARON GRIPSTEIN [*Wonderingly*]
"Riffoni Vittorio; *La Sera*"?   But I can't see a journalist now.

OMAR
So I told him, Effendi.   But he says his business burns.

BARON GRIPSTEIN [*Fretfully*]
Yes, I know.   But tell him I've already sent the press the list of guests.

LIVIA [*Shocked*]
Eh? . . .
   [*Grimly*]
And now, I suppose, he expects the menu.

BARON GRIPSTEIN
Ah, yes.
   [*To* OMAR]
Give him a menu.

LIVIA
No, no!

11

BARON GRIPSTEIN [*To* OMAR]
Not a real menu, of course, with a water-colour. A copy.

OMAR
I understand, Effendi.
   [*Salaams and exit.*]

LIVIA
Oh, Baron, you are hopeless. Why did you send out the list of guests?

BARON GRIPSTEIN
To seal our position, of course.

LIVIA
Considering the Queen's visit has precisely that gracious object, you might have left the publication to the Court chronicler.

BARON GRIPSTEIN
He would have published only the dinner-guests, not the reception list.
   [*Re-enter* OMAR.]

OMAR
I have given him the menu, Effendi, but he stands like a pillar.

LIVIA [*Angrily*]
He won't go?

OMAR
Not without a word to Baron Gripstein.

12

LIVIA

You see! Now that you have conceded the creature the menu, he renews his hope of an interview. . . .

[*To* OMAR]

Tell him the Baron has nothing to say for publication.

[OMAR *salaams and exit again.*]

BARON GRIPSTEIN

I suppose because the paper is now mine, the fellow thinks——

LIVIA [*Shocked*]

You've bought the *Sera?* The Socialist rag that is egging on the peasants to claim the land!

BARON GRIPSTEIN [*Smiling*]

That is why Cazotti gave me the hint to buy it up.

LIVIA

Oh, I see.

BARON GRIPSTEIN

Yes. Its effect on the peasants one does not take seriously, especially as they can't read. But it began running a translation of a boycotted American book by the Notorious Nicholas Stone called *The Nemesis of Nationality*, which urged that in this latter-day world of heavy armaments, nationality is a luxury beyond our means. Even the middle-classes, groaning under the post-war taxation, began to ask, Does patriotism pay?

LIVIA

You were quite right to stop the paper.

13

BARON GRIPSTEIN

No, no, *cara*—we haven't stopped it. Under the new editorship *La Sera* can be made a respectable property —respectable in every sense. We haven't even stopped the Nicholas Stone serial. But I understand that by a little judicious mistranslation, it is coming to a *sounder conclusion*. Ha! ha! ha! Not a bad joke, Livia.

LIVIA

But surely, Baron, that's not fair to the American author!

[*Re-enter* OMAR.]

OMAR

The pillar still stands, Effendi.

LIVIA

What! Why have you not thrown him out?

OMAR

I took counsel of Signor Brio. But he feared, with the crowd round the house——

BARON GRIPSTEIN

Brio is quite right. We cannot have a scene to-night. Tell the man I'll see him in the morning. . . .

[*Apologetically to* LIVIA]

One *must* see journalists—they have such sharp quills.

LIVIA

Not when one owns their papers.

BARON GRIPSTEIN

The same man writes on other papers—even opposition papers.

LIVIA
How horrible!

BARON GRIPSTEIN
They are no worse than barristers.
　　[*To* OMAR]
What are you waiting for?

OMAR
For an instruction. The man will surely again refuse
to go without a word from you. Shall we throw him
into the crowd?

LIVIA
Of course.

BARON GRIPSTEIN [*Agitated*]
No, no, Livia. And we *must* get rid of him before
Her Majesty arrives. Lucky I came down so early.
Tell him, Omar, I will give him five minutes at
once———
　　[OMAR *salaams and exit*]
And his dismissal from the paper to-morrow. And
you will have five minutes to change to the diamond
necklace.

LIVIA
I had better employ them in inspecting the dinner-
table.
　　[*Goes to central folding doors. Pauses*]
Will you never remember———?

15

BARON GRIPSTEIN [*Rushing to open the doors*]
I beg your pardon.
>[*There is again a glimpse of the rose-crowned table,* BRIO, *and the hovering lackeys.*]

LIVIA
And don't forget on the other hand that you must make no special fuss of the Queen, beyond our going down to receive her. . . . And not a word to this interviewer about Her Majesty or ourselves—especially in a paper of your own. I don't know why Society nowadays puts itself on the level of dancers or cinema clowns that live only by the breath of the mob.
>[*Exit as* OMAR *ushers in* RIFFONI VITTORIO, *taking his hat and stick. The newcomer is a magnetic figure in the prime of early manhood with a long, powerful, clean-shaven face and the eyes of a fanatic. His clothes, though he is not in evening dress, are sufficiently well-cut and brushed to account for* OMAR'S *indecision. In his hand he holds a copy of the menu.*]

BARON GRIPSTEIN [*Very cordially*]
Ah, Signor——
>[*Looking at card still in his hand*]
Riffoni. I was sorry to be unable to receive you immeditely. And even now— —
>[*Takes out his watch.*]

RIFFONI
The five minutes, Baron, will be ample.
16

BARON GRIPSTEIN
Ah! Won't you take a seat?

RIFFONI
Thank you.
  [*Sits.*]

BARON GRIPSTEIN
I fear we must not touch upon the honour Her Majesty is doing me.

RIFFONI
I never meant to touch upon it.

BARON GRIPSTEIN [*Disconcerted*]
No—precisely—er—do you smoke?

RIFFONI
I neither smoke nor drink.

BARON GRIPSTEIN
A paragon among us Christians! Then we can go on talking here.
  [*Sits.*]
For of course the room in which I receive Her Majesty——

RIFFONI
Naturally.

BARON GRIPSTEIN
Not that anybody ever smokes in this room even when Her Majesty is not here. The Baroness Sigismondo, my daughter-in-law, who was a maid of honour, learnt repugnance to tobacco from her royal mistress, and

17

even I am not allowed to taint our ancestral tapestries. It makes a difficulty when her aunt, the Grand Duchess of Carelia, who is fond of cigarettes——

RIFFONI [*Abruptly*]
I have come to talk about Salaret!

BARON GRIPSTEIN [*Startled*]
Eh?

RIFFONI
About Salaret.

BARON GRIPSTEIN
Salaret! What is Salaret?

RIFFONI
You don't know the greatest man in Valdania?

BARON GRIPSTEIN
Oh, it is a man.

RIFFONI
And the greatest in the world—except Nicholas Stone.

BARON GRIPSTEIN
Ah, a Pacifist! . . .
    [*Rising*]
Excuse me, are you still on the staff of the *Sera?*

RIFFONI
Of course not. I was kicked out with Salaret when the paper changed hands. Did I give you my old card? I should have given you this.
    [*Produces another card.*]

18

BARON GRIPSTEIN [*Taking it*]
"Honorary Secretary of the Scaletta Society for the Prevention of Cruelty to Animals."

RIFFONI [*With a grim smile*]
Editors included. At first we thought the *Sera* had been acquired by its new editor, Oroscobonetti. But we have just traced the proprietorship to you.

BARON GRIPSTEIN
I see. But you take a strange tone if you wish me to put you back.

RIFFONI
Me? What do *I* matter? I was born with plenty of money and never clogged my wings with a wife. But Professor Salaret was a child of poverty and has fifty-five years and eight children to carry. His wife's money enabled him to give up his professorship and devote himself to Socialistic literature; but it was merely an annuity, and when she died, he had only this editorship to rely on. Of course I've done what I could, but the paper had already swallowed up most of my funds, and now his children are practically starving.

BARON GRIPSTEIN [*Moved*]
Poor things!

RIFFONI
The eldest son, Guido, who is just of age, is most brilliant—a real genius for chemistry. But had it not been for the generosity of Komak, a fellow-student,

19

he would not have been able to remain at the Technical
College.

BARON GRIPSTEIN
A genius for chemistry! But it is what our country
needs.

RIFFONI
She needs his father more. Salaret must be restored
to his editorship.

BARON GRIPSTEIN
But of course! I knew nothing of these changes in
detail. But I can easily find another billet for Oros-
connetti, or whatever his name is.

RIFFONI
Ah, thank you. I expected to meet a monster and I
find a man.

BARON GRIPSTEIN
Capitalists as well as editors should come under the
protection of your Society.
    [*Holds out his hand*]
And if you would like a subscription to it——

RIFFONI
How good of you!

BARON GRIPSTEIN
Of course this friend of yours will edit it in the new
spirit.

RIFFONI [*Drops his hand as if stung*]
What! As a bourgeoise Cazotti organ!

BARON GRIPSTEIN
As a popular Liberal evening paper.

RIFFONI
How dare you insult the Master? Salaret who has given Valdania the new vision, whose whole life——!
    [*Chokes with indignation.*]

BARON GRIPSTEIN
You surely don't expect me to pay a man to saw away the legs of my chair?

RIFFONI
If it will prevent your own legs being sawn away. As Pacifists, Salaret and I have never preached violence. We have thought that the workers, being the overwhelming majority, had only to return a Labour Parliament to bring about the dictation of the proletariat. But if you destroy our organ, if you cut out our tongue—oh, don't you see that to take away free speech is to deny the right of citizens to reform their State from within, is to make us foreigners whose only weapon is force?

BARON GRIPSTEIN
But who denies you free speech? Even my major-domo stands opposed to my politics. Start another organ.

RIFFONI
But where can we find a capitalist?

BARON GRIPSTEIN
Ha! ha! ha! Excuse my merriment. So even to

destroy capital you need a capitalist! What about the capitalist I bought it from?

RIFFONI
There was no such capitalist. I thought I explained that Salaret had started the paper himself while his wife was alive, and that afterwards I helped him all I could.

BARON GRIPSTEIN
But what about the money I paid for it?

RIFFONI
Salaret had to use that to pay off the printers' arrears.

BARON GRIPSTEIN
But I took those over, if I remember. Anyhow, Salaret sold me his own paper, and you accuse me of sacking him!

RIFFONI
He had to sell—else the printers would have stopped it all the same. But he had no idea that the buyer was your agent, and he fully expected to be kept on as editor.

BARON GRIPSTEIN
When he had failed to make it pay? . . . How much did he owe the printers?

RIFFONI
How should I know?

22

BARON GRIPSTEIN
You sank your fortune in the paper, yet you never saw a balance-sheet?

RIFFONI
A balance-sheet? Salaret is a saint and a martyr!

BARON GRIPSTEIN [*Drily*]
And a true Socialist—willing to share your last lira.

RIFFONI
How dare you! It was a privilege for me.

BARON GRIPSTEIN
Anyhow, even with your money and the money he married, he could not make the paper pay.

RIFFONI
That was not his fault. The price had to be doubled— printing is so dear nowadays.

BARON GRIPSTEIN
But why is printing so dear? See how these Trade Unions cut one another's throats! So the proletariat won't pay for your ideas?

RIFFONI
They can't afford to.

BARON GRIPSTEIN
Not four soldi? But think what they spend on cinemas and cigarettes! No, no, Signor, it is clear your ideas are not wanted.

23

RIFFONI
Not wanted?

BARON GRIPSTEIN
Whatever is wanted is paid for.

RIFFONI
A pretty touchstone!

BARON GRIPSTEIN
The only scientific one. Face the facts, my friend.

RIFFONI
Then—do you suppose *you* are wanted to this extent?
  [*Waves his arm round the room.*]

BARON GRIPSTEIN [*Complacently*]
To all appearance. Do not forget what Valdania was
before I took her in hand. Hardly an industry, hardly
a railway, a mass of peasantry exploited by the boyars.
I have done more for the proletariat than all your
Salarets.

RIFFONI
On the contrary. You are destroying their old feudal
life. The boyar was a brother, if too much of a
big brother. To-day in these industries of yours every
man is for himself and the devil for them all. Mother
earth is paved over, masses slave or starve unnoted.
And while a Salaret is thrown on the scrap-heap, some
brainless prodigal son squanders in a night what would
keep the Master and his family going for a year.
What a system!

24

BARON GRIPSTEIN
With all its faults it is the only system that works.
If the son is prodigal, it means the father has saved
and slaved—and if he had not been able to pass on
his savings to his son, would he have worked so hard?

RIFFONI
So that is humanity's last word—to produce not for
consumption, but for profit! And to distribute so
wickedly that your lazy luxurious childless ladies are
living off mothers of the people—hardly recognisable
as of the same species—with infants at their wizened
breasts and a ragged brood at their skirts! O the
cry of the people—cannot you hear it day and night
like the moaning of a wintry sea?

BARON GRIPSTEIN
The last time I heard it was at the races, when it was
jubilant over the victory of my filly, Margherita.

RIFFONI
They must have *some* outlet, these helots of our reeking alleys. Ah, Baron, why not help us to build a
world of justice and common joyous labour? Believe
me, you would be happier than in this monstrous and
brutal opulence.

BARON GRIPSTEIN [*Outraged*]
Brutal? And my hospitals, soup-kitchens, orphan-
ages, free milk centres——?

25

RIFFONI
Blackmail to ward off revolution or to keep your footing in society.

BARON GRIPSTEIN
Your five minutes are at an end.
 [*Moves coldly away.*]

RIFFONI
You asked me to face the facts. Do you suppose people come to you for your beautiful eyes? Even Queens, they say, need money.

BARON GRIPSTEIN
It is a scandalous suggestion—go, go!

RIFFONI
Even if Her Majesty takes no money from you for herself, she takes it for her charities.

BARON GRIPSTEIN
And has she not given to mine?

RIFFONI
You may be charitable in yourself, it remains true that, in the words of Karl Marx, the thing you represent face to face with me has no heart in its breast. And do you call it charity to give away what you never feel the absence of? Have you sacrificed a single petal of your bed of roses? You may throw the poor the thousands, you wallow in the millions.

BARON GRIPSTEIN
And divided among the poor, what would my millions

amount to? Not fifty lire per head. Kept together, they create industries, promote commerce, foster art. You, like Montesquieu's savage, would cut down the tree to gather the fruit.

RIFFONI
No! But I would divide it equally. Look at the fruit on this menu alone!

BARON GRIPSTEIN
And would that equalise happiness? My butler's boys came back from the war, but my eldest-born rots in the ravines of Bosnavina.
[*Falls into a chair and covers his eyes.*]

RIFFONI
I am sorry—but paupers too lost their sons. When I was a lad my little brother was drowned in the lake, but my father did not consider that this was a reason for eating more than his neighbour.
[*Tears up his copy of the menu.*]

BARON GRIPSTEIN [*Hardly listening*]
And my blinded Sigismondo! Will you cut out one of *your* eyes and give him optical equality? Ah, Signor, you make so much of poverty because you have never known it. Otherwise you would have known that bodily hunger is not so horrible as this gnawing of the heart.

RIFFONI
Baron Gripstein is hardly an authority on hunger.

BARON GRIPSTEIN
Is he not ?
    [*Springs up*]
And do you suppose he inherited this?
    [*Waving arm round*]
No, Signor, I was born in one of the reeking alleys
you speak of—no, no, not here, in Germany—and
my mother was one of those women of the people,
torn between the babe at the breast and the brood
at the skirt.   There were ten of us, never knowing
whether father would bring home bread or not, yet
every Friday evening——
    [*Pauses abruptly.*]

RIFFONI [*Interested*]
Every Friday evening——

BARON GRIPSTEIN
Yes—trumpet it to your papers if you like—it was
the Jew-street I was born in.   But the Sabbath hal-
lowed it with peace.   Ah, I have never been so happy
since.
    [*Drops back into his chair and covers his eyes
    again.*]

RIFFONI [*Half moved, half sneering*]
A pity you don't try to return to that happiness.

BARON GRIPSTEIN
On the road of life there is no returning.   But do you
think I could bear to go on treading it, if I didn't
still believe in God?

28

RIFFONI

God! Ah, there we have it. God! The belief that keeps this devil's system safe! That takes away our responsibility, saps our effort——

[*Reenter* LIVIA *by the folding doors.*]

LIVIA

Not finished yet? You seem to have agitated the Baron. Please go.

RIFFONI

Not till the Baron has agreed to my terms.

LIVIA

Your terms?

[SHE *goes haughtily to the bell.*]

BARON GRIPSTEIN [*Looking up wearily*]

Don't ring, Livia. The Signor will go quietly. He knows that the Queen is expected, that gendarmes lurk everywhere, and that at a movement of my finger he would be arrested.

RIFFONI

Gendarmes everywhere! Ha! ha! ha! So this is your beloved sovereign.

[*Enter* OMAR.]

BARON GRIPSTEIN [*Perturbed*]

Nobody rang.

OMAR

No, Effendi. But I thought that with the pillar still

29

standing, you would wish to know that the Prime
Minister's carriage has reached the courtyard.

LIVIA
Already?

BARON GRIPSTEIN
He told me he would come early to get a private chat
on the Bosnavinian Loan. . . . Thank you, Omar,
you acted rightly. And will you see the Signor out?

RIFFONI
But the Prime Minister is the very person I wish to
meet!

LIVIA
This is outrageous. Omar, will you tell Colonel
Molp——?

RIFFONI
Pause, Baroness, before you kick me out into a crowd
composed not merely of idolaters of your goddess, but
of worshippers of Salaret, to whom you and yours are
but parasites upon Labour. And even to the idolaters,
the thought of their girl-queen inveigled here by a
Jew-financier——!

BARON GRIPSTEIN [*Hastily*]
Omar, why are you not escorting the Prime Minister?
[OMAR *salaams and exit. To* LIVIA]
Cazotti will deal with him.

RIFFONI
I hope so.   For whatever Cazotti lacks, it is not
prudence.

OMAR [*Re-appearing at door*]
His Excellency, the Prime Minister.
>   [COUNT CAZOTTI *advances and kisses the* BARON-
>   ESS'S *hand. His short frame is tending to corpu-
>   lence, but his conscious Napoleonic head is free
>   from signs of spiritual growth. He wears many
>   decorations.*]

LIVIA
Delighted to see you so early.

BARON GRIPSTEIN [*Shaking hands*]
But where is the dear Countess?

CAZOTTI [*Smilingly*]
You know she prefers coming in Her Majesty's train.

BARON GRIPSTEIN
Ah, yes, of course, always so devoted to duty.

CAZOTTI [*Linking his arm in the* BARON'S]
And now, if the Baroness will excuse me, let us talk
of my investments.   You see the bonds at Amster-
dam——
>   [*Pauses abruptly as he becomes aware of* RIFFONI,
>   *who bows ironically.*]

BARON GRIPSTEIN
I am so sorry, your Excellency, but this man insists
on meeting you.

CAZOTTI
Eh?

LIVIA
We must humbly apologise. But you arrived before
we could have him removed.

BARON GRIPSTEIN
He is taking advantage of the mob outside to black-
mail me into reinstating the old editor of the *Sera*.
There's his card.

CAZOTTI [*Perusing it*]
Oh, that gaol-bird!

RIFFONI
BARON GRIPSTEIN } Gaol-bird?
LIVIA

CAZOTTI
Curiously enough the Minister of the Interior showed
me his dossier only this morning.

RIFFONI
I challenge you to detail it.

CAZOTTI
You deny you have been in prison? Why, you only
just escaped execution!

BARON GRIPSTEIN
My God!

RIFFONI
Don't be alarmed. It was only for scattering Pacifist

32

poems from my areoplane during the Bosnavinian war. My father's *Songs of Brotherhood*.

CAZOTTI
We all believe in brotherhood. But that was not the moment.

RIFFONI
It never is. And so our streets are filled with noseless torsos, like the wreckage of ancient sculpture come to grotesque life. But if you think we shall for ever go to the shambles at the bidding of old men with shrivelled hearts and fly-blown brains——!

LIVIA
How dare you speak like that to the Prime Minister?

CAZOTTI
Oh, I'm used to it, dear Signora. The Labour Party in the Chamber is not large but it is vivacious.

RIFFONI
Shall I tell you something else that happened to me in the air? I heard one day through the roar of my machine the hymns of both armies ascending to heaven in rival requests for victory. In the absence of God, I determined to answer their foolish prayer myself by giving them not victory but peace.

BARON GRIPSTEIN
A blasphemous lunatic!

RIFFONI [*Drily*]
Whose ambition is to leave the world a little saner

33

than he found it. I tell you I will make a new heaven and a new earth—by making heaven *upon* earth. My father could only dream the dream—I, by realising it, shall best avenge his murder.

BARON GRIPSTEIN [*Shocked again*]
His murder?

CAZOTTI
Your father was not murdered. He died of heart failure while on sentry duty at the Palace.

RIFFONI
To conscript a man of that age, and expose him in that frost!

CAZOTTI
We must all die for our country when duty calls.

RIFFONI
No! Our country must die for us when duty calls. Nationalism is the enemy.

CAZOTTI
Aha! Nicholas Stone! . . . With these Pacifist sentiments of yours, how do you explain your behaviour on your release from the military prison? You sought to revenge yourself on my person, and, not finding me in the carriage, you insulted my wife and assaulted my coachman.

LIVIA
Ah, I remember the case. The poor Countess was a witness.

34

RIFFONI
A false one.

CAZOTTI [*Raising his fist*]
You dare——!

RIFFONI
Ah, now *you* will do the assaulting.
    [CAZOTTI's *arm drops*]
Your coachman was lashing his horses brutally because they refused to pass a piece of paper—perhaps
    [*Smilingly*]
it was a page of the *Sera*. You know, Baroness, how
horses yearn dumbly to us through their great tragic
eyes. When I remonstrated with the brute—the real
brute—he turned his whip on me. I seized the thong
and was pulling him out of his seat when your per-
jured police came up.

CAZOTTI
The judge saw the facts otherwise. . . . No sooner
were you released than you began a series of violent
articles in the *Sera*.

BARON GRIPSTEIN
And he told me he never preached violence.

RIFFONI
A violent article is not one preaching violence. Not
even prison and injustice could destroy my faith in
the force of reason. Rotten houses fall of themselves.
A gnat's bite will kill a man whose blood is purulent.
And a society which makes it a crime to proclaim
35

brotherhood, which would have shot me dead, had I not happened to have saved a brother-airman, though at the cost of sending his assailant crashing down in cinders—ugh!

[*Covers his eyes*]

Oh, how could I bear to live under an economic system which makes such things inevitable?

CAZOTTI

It is to save you from living under it—so far at least as Valdania is concerned—that the Minister of the Interior has just signed an order for your explusion.

RIFFONI
What!

LIVIA
Bravo!

[*All speaking simultaneously.*]

BARON GRIPSTEIN [*Rubbing hands*]
Aha!

CAZOTTI
You will pursue your quest for brotherhood and economic equality in some other country.

RIFFONI
I am to be expelled from Valdania?

CAZOTTI
Tomorrow morning. May I advise you to take advantage of this early information by hurrying home to wind up your affairs?

36

RIFFONI
And that is your Democratic Constitution!

CAZOTTI
Democracy means that every man in Valdania has a
vote. You will not be in Valdania. It is very simple.

RIFFONI
As simple as the way you crawled by slimy spirals
to the summit of power. And under what law does
the State exile its citizens?

CAZOTTI
The first law of nature—the law of self protection.

RIFFONI [*With set face and clenched fists*]
Ah, the party of force was right after all! . . . So,
unable to meet our arguments, you capitalist bullies,
not content to cut out our organ of speech, cut us
out of the realm altogether.

CAZOTTI
Us?

RIFFONI
Salaret and me.

CAZOTTI
Oh, we are not deporting Salaret. He is not dangerous.

RIFFONI [*Dazed*]
Salaret is not dangerous?

37

OMAR [*At door* L., *announcing*]
His Highness, the Duke D'Azollo.
    [*Exit.*]
    [*The* DUKE, *magnificently bestarred and berib-
    boned, comes tottering and peering in. Age has
    wrinkled his fine features and reduced his snowy
    mane, but his smile is still fascinating.* HE *kisses*
    LIVIA'S *hand with the romantic courtesy of an
    earlier generation.*]

LIVIA
Delighted to see you looking so well. . . .
    [*Ironically*]
The Duchess, I fear, has a headache.

DUKE D'AZOLLO
As you divine, alas!

BARON GRIPSTEIN [*Shakes his hand*]
I am so sorry.

DUKE D'AZOLLO
If it abates, she hopes to come in for the reception.

BARON GRIPSTEIN
So good of Her Highness to honour our humble home.

DUKE D'AZOLLO [*Peering*]
Ah, is that our perpetual Premier?
    [*Shakes hands with* CAZOTTI, *then stumbles on*
    RIFFONI]
Well, well, Vittorio, who would expect to meet *you*
here?
    [*Wrings his hand warmly.*]

38

CAZOTTI [*Taken aback*]
You know him?

DUKE D'AZOLLO
Am I not President of his Society for the Prevention of Cruelty to Animals? Or have I been superseded, Vittorio?

RIFFONI [*Coldly*]
The Duchess sent me your resignation when I was imprisoned for assaulting Count Cazotti's coachman.

DUKE D'AZOLLO
But that was very wrong of you, Vittorio. How could the coachman help his master's misgovernment? It is really very Christian of Cazotti to meet you like this. In future, my young friend, stick to your delightful articles.

CAZOTTI
You approve of his articles!

DUKE D'AZOLLO
What can be more digestive after a good dinner than a spirited denunciation of the sinfulness of eating it? A Riffoni article with one's coffee is better than cognac.

CAZOTTI [*Sarcastically*]
If our host had only known, he would have put one on the menu.

DUKE D'AZOLLO
Tut! Tut! Our young friend is merely developing your ideas more logically.

39

CAZOTTI
My ideas?

DUKE D'AZOLLO
Didn't your Government take possession of my finest
farm for a munition factory? As for your income-
tax, it is only expropriation under another name.
Your Finance Minister simply ruins my other creditors.
He! he! he! And this pretence of not being socialistic is the sillier because it takes in the masses, and
thus you despoil us without appeasing them.

BARON GRIPSTEIN
There is something in that.

DUKE D'AZOLLO
And then isn't the State going to own my pictures?

CAZOTTI
Only by your generosity.

DUKE D'AZOLLO
Not at all—by my dear Baron's.
    [*Claps* GRIPSTEIN'S *shoulder laughingly.* *The*
    BARON *makes deprecatory Oriental gestures.*]
When he redeemed them from my creditors, he
allowed me only a life-interest.

CAZOTTI
At any rate the State does not confiscate them.

DUKE D'AZOLLO
It confiscated alcohol-values in America. Everywhere in Europe it comes between the house-proprie-

tor and his natural rent.   Ah, it is clear the heyday of
private property is over.

RIFFONI
Bravo!

CAZOTTI
I am so sorry to see the ex-Regent of Valdania coquet-
ting with Communism.

DUKE D'AZOLLO
But why should not the State be run in peace-time
with the same common devotion as in war-time?

RIFFONI
Bravissimo!

CAZOTTI
That intensity of co-operation is possible only under
deadly danger.   Like deathbed repentance, it does not
survive recovery.

LIVIA
And even under danger, Duke, it is not to be relied
on.   When I worked in the hospital, I found men who
had mutilated themselves to escape service.

CAZOTTI
Exactly.   As I found profiteers who had mutilated
the State.   Even the patriotic workers sent in their
bills afterwards—   Ha! ha! ha!   My dentist confessed to me that when he was first mobilised to look
after the soldiers' teeth, he worked thirteen hours a
day till his fellow-dentists laughed him out of it.   Then
41

he became a slacker like the others. No, no, Duke, State-interest cannot vie with self-interest.

DUKE D'AZOLLO
Yet self as the central principle of society is hardly compatible with our religion.

RIFFONI [*Drily*]
Nor did the early Christians possess private steam-yachts and picture galleries. St. Francis defined theft as keeping anything somebody else needed more.

DUKE D'AZOLLO [*Laughingly*]
This terrible Vittorio. He's not content I should coquet with Communism. He wants a marriage on the spot—a marriage of inconvenience! My galleries —you have already heard they are to go to the pro-letariat, though it prefers its pictures moving. But what would you do with my steam-yacht? Eh? Have fishermen spill their catches on its carpets and spit out their quids on its painted panels? Nothing is ready yet for your new system, my dear Vittorio. Give us time. Rome was not destroyed in a day. Life is compromise.

RIFFONI
Never! Life is sacrifice!

CAZOTTI [*To the* DUKE]
I beg you not to engage your friend in argument now. He has to go before the Queen arrives.

DUKE D'AZOLLO [*Turning to* BARON]
He is not staying to dinner?

42

BARON GRIPSTEIN [*Embarrassed*]
He—I——

LIVIA [*Feigning a smile*]
Can't you see, Duke, by his clothes?

DUKE D'AZOLLO [*Peering at* RIFFONI]
Eh? My sight is getting even worse than my memory!
    [*Feeling in his pockets*]
I must have left my glasses in my overcoat.
    [*Moves to door* L.]

BARON GRIPSTEIN
Let me send down for them.

DUKE D'AZOLLO
No, no, my pockets are still private property, eh,
Vittorio? He! he! he!
    [*At door pauses and turns*]
Talking of glasses, Vittorio, you Utopians remind
me of a passage in an American author named—
named——
    [*Twiddles his thumbs.*]

RIFFONI
Nicholas Stone?

DUKE D'AZOLLO
No, no. *Santa Maria,* my memory! . . . Ah, Mark
Twain! He went up Mont Blanc by telescope. That's
how you Socialists go up your Mont Rouge—at a
peep. Aha! but wait till you are actually among the
crevasses and glaciers——

43

RIFFONI
We shall be roped together.

DUKE D'AZOLLO [*Moving back into room, prepared to argue*]
And together you will tumble.

CAZOTTI [*Almost pushing him out*]
You are forgetting your glasses.

DUKE D'AZOLLO
Santa Maria, I forget everything—except my manners.
  [*Exit.*]

CAZOTTI
The old sinner. How he can mention that yacht of
his without blushing——!

BARON GRIPSTEIN
Oh, but that's all over now. We go to early Mass
together.

CAZOTTI
It was high time—for *him,* I mean. . . . And now,
Signor Riffoni, now that we have considerately concealed your painful position from your friend, the
Duke, you will kindly take your leave before he discovers it.

RIFFONI
Take my leave? When it is my last evening in Valdanian society! No, no, let me see everybody—it is
my last chance.

BARON GRIPSTEIN
You surely do not propose to be here when the
Queen——!

RIFFONI
But I've only seen her caracoling in a colonel's uniform, goading us on to murder. A more intimate
impression——

LIVIA
This is the climax

RIFFONI
The crown, you should say. Will she wear it? I
have often wondered how the same crown fits all our
successive sovereigns. I suppose their heads swell
uniformly.

CAZOTTI
Stop this fooling and go!
    [*Takes out his watch*]
I give you sixty seconds to clear out.
    [RIFFONI *drops into a chair and folds his arms.*]

BARON GRIPSTEIN
Oh, your Excellency, you should not have told him of
his expulsion.

CAZOTTI
It was an indiscretion, I admit. But there are ways
of expulsion even from a salon.

45

BARON GRIPSTEIN
But he has his gang outside. Her Majesty must not
be agitated.

LIVIA
Don't be so timid, Baron. The man cannot be here
when the Queen——

RIFFONI
And has not every Valdanian the right to appeal to
his sovereign?

CAZOTTI
So that's your game, is it, to appeal against your
banishment?

RIFFONI
As if I would submit my natural right to the caprice
of a pampered young woman. No!
    [*Springs up*]
Let us two come face to face—the despised and re-
jected of Valdania with its idol and glory, the lowly
peace-lover with the swaggering Amazon who drew
the sword of Alpastroom!

BARON GRIPSTEIN
But she is *not* such an antithesis—she is rather——

CAZOTTI
Fifty-eight, fifty-nine, sixty!
    [*Snaps watch-case*]
You permit me to ring, Baroness?
46

LIVIA
Of course.

BARON GRIPSTEIN
For God's sake!
    [CAZOTTI *rings. Enter* OMAR.]

CAZOTTI
Ask Colonel Molp to step in!
    [RIFFONI *sits down defiantly again. There is a
    tense silence during which the* BARON *opens his
    mouth agitatedly several times to address* CAZOTTI
    or RIFFONI, *but fails to say anything, and ends by
    wiping his brow.* COLONEL MOLP *enters door* L.,
    *a rather rough-hewn figure in evening dress with
    medals.* HE *bows to the company*]
Colonel Molp, we wish you to prevent this man
leaving the house——
    [RIFFONI *gives a murmur of surprise*]
till Her Majesty is safely at dinner. Keep him under
arrest and subsequently under observation till he is
deported.

MOLP
Yes, Excellency. I know his record.

RIFFONI
I know yours. Janissary, spy, denouncer, *agent pro-
vocateur*——

MOLP [*Imperturbably*]
This way, Signor.
    [*Motions towards door.* RIFFONI *with a sudden*
47

*dart the other way opens the window, letting in
the confused sounds of a mob.* MOLP *veers round.*]

RIFFONI
Back, or I appeal to our followers!

BARON GRIPSTEIN [*Besides himself, to* CAZOTTI]
I warned your Excellency——

CAZOTTI [*To* RIFFONI]
Close the window and you shall remain.
[RIFFONI *closes the window with a triumphant
smile*]
Bring in your men, Colonel, they will cover him up
from the Queen.

MOLP
Or draw her eyes to him. Her Majesty hates seeing
me much more my men. She refused our escort.

CAZOTTI
But suppose he is armed! . . . If he moves a suspicious finger, use your dagger—not your pistol.

BARON GRIPSTEIN
God of Israel!

RIFFONI
You would murder me?

CAZOTTI
Would you have us accused of collusion in the murder
of the Queen?

RIFFONI
I have no weapon except a fountain-pen. Do you
48

suppose I would sacrifice my destruction of your whole
social order to vengeance on your paltry Margherita?
The peasant must have the land, the workman the
industries, the country peace—that's what I shall tell
your royal Juggernaut.

CAZOTTI
With your fountain-pen. One word in Her Majesty's
hearing and Salaret shares your exile.

RIFFONI
You brute!
> [HE *collapses on the cushioned window-seat.* MOLP
> *takes up his post vigilantly beside him. Re-enter
> the* DUKE D'AZOLLO, *still peering through eye-
> glasses.* HE *brushes by the astonished* MOLP.]

DUKE D'AZOLLO
Ah, Vittorio glad you haven't run away yet. Because
I *should* like to hear what you will do with my steam-
yacht.

RIFFONI
I shall come back in her—with the Red Flag flying.

DUKE D'AZOLLO
Back? You are leaving Valdania?

RIFFONI
Needs must when the devil drives

DUKE D'AZOLLO
But where does he drive you?

49

RIFFONI
Up Mont Rouge.

DUKE D'AZOLLO
He! he! he! You are not the first whom the devil
has taken up a high mountain. But can you really
read Karl Marx? I'd sooner be expropriated. What
does he mean
    [*Sits down beside him for a long talk*]
by all that algebraical stuff about surplus-value?. . .

OMAR [*Announcing at door*]
Their Excellencies, the Viscount and Viscountess
Palestra.
    [*A pompous couple enters.*]

LIVIA
So glad you could come.
    [*The* VISCOUNT *kisses her hand.*]

BARON GRIPSTEIN
Welcome to my humble home. . . .
    [*Sotto voce to the* VISCOUNT]
I managed to allot you those Bosnavinian bonds.
    [*The couple passes on to greet* CAZOTTI.]

OMAR
Signor and Signora da Grasso.
    [*An elderly saturnine gentleman appears with
    a bouncing middle-aged beauty, whose natural
    charms, though considerable, do not conceal art.*]

50

LIVIA [*As her hand is kissed*]
So glad to see you back in Scaletta. Your peasants
must have quieted down.

ESTER DA GRASSO
Yes, my husband soon stopped that nonsense of their
wanting our land.

LIVIA
Why, what did he do?

BARON GRIPSTEIN
Don't tell us, please.
[*Quietly and with an uneasy look towards* VIT-
TORIO, *who is, however, engrossed in his argument
with the* DUKE]
The Socialists might hear of it.
[*Lowering his voice further*]
Even the Queen is capable of siding with the peasants.

ESTER DA GRASSO
I have no patience with what I hear of her.

BARON GRIPSTEIN [*Shocked and alarmed*]
Sh! Sh!

OMAR [*Announcing*]
His Excellency, Marshal Roxo.

BARON GRIPSTEIN [*Darting forward in relief*]
Ah!
[LIVIA *checks him with a glance and* HE *returns
sheepishly to her side. The* MARSHAL, *an ailing
veteran, peppered with medals and orders, comes*

51

forward rheumatically to kiss her hand. The DA
GRASSOS *join the* PALESTRAS *and* CAZOTTI.]

LIVIA
Delighted to see you about again, Marshal; by the
way, have you your slip?
[HE *produces a scrap of paper*]
Ha! As I thought. But I'm afraid the Duchess
D'Azollo is indisposed.

ROXO
All the better—no, I don't mean that. But I shan't
have to give her the wrong arm.

CAZOTTI [*Advancing to shake hands*]
Ah, Marshal, how goes the enemy?

ROXO
As you see—not formidable enough to prevent my
sortie.

CAZOTTI
You are a wonderful man—we shall yet see you head-
ing a new campaign.

ROXO
Not while you remain Prime Minister!

CAZOTTI
Ha! ha! ha! And the Queen thinks me so warlike.
But the Bosnavinian business finished me. The old
conquerors got loot, we moderns get income-tax! Not
to mention loans to the conquered! I bless my stars

52

that Rolmenia didn't call your bluff and fly to liberate Bosnavina.

ROXO
It wasn't me Rolmenia was frightened of, it was poor Marrobio. But now that she's got him safely assassinated——

OMAR [*Announcing*]
Their Highnesses, Prince and Princess Gondaroff.

ROXO [*To* CAZOTTI, *as the youngish* PRINCE *and* PRINCESS *advance to be greeted*]
Bosnavinians here?

CAZOTTI
You see the effect of the loan. But they are not the only Bosnavinians who prefer Scaletta and our culture, though the Queen fusses so over the compulsory Valdanian in their schools.

OMAR [*Announcing*]
His Excellency, the Rolmenian Minister!
    [*A gorgeously uniformed and subtle-looking ancient advances.*]

CAZOTTI [*Sotto voce to* ROXO *as the Minister is being welcomed*]
Oh, do go and let him pump you on the army.

ROXO
Shall I let out it's strong or weak?

CAZOTTI
Strong, but undermined by Socialism.

53

ROXO
But that's the truth!

CAZOTTI
As if he will believe it!
[ROXO *goes up to greet the Rolmenian Minister as
he leaves the* BARONESS.]

OMAR
Her Excellency, the Countess Villop.

LIVIA [*As the* COUNTESS *enters*]
How good of you to come!

BARON GRIPSTEIN
Ah, Countess, there is no one whose presence in my
humble home——
[*Cheering from outside penetrates even through the
closed window*]
Ah, Her Majesty! Excuse me! Come, Livia.

LIVIA
There is plenty of time.
[*Turns to* PRINCESS GONDAROFF, *who has not left
her*]
Yes, Princess, your *Bora* is not a nice wind. But in
revenge your summers——
[*Louder cheering.*]

BARON GRIPSTEIN [*Glancing anxiously at* RIF-
FONI]
Livia! We shall be late.
[*Enter* OMAR R.]

54

OMAR
Her Majesty is arriving.

BARON GRIPSTEIN
I told you we should be late.

LIVIA [*Taking his arm and whispering*]
Compose yourself!
> [THEY *go out, not without an uneasy backward glance of the* BARON'S *at* RIFFONI, *who is still in discussion with the* DUKE, *both oblivious of the watching* MOLP. OMAR *closes the door and disappears.*]

ESTER DA GRASSO [*Sotto voce to* COUNTESS VILLOP]
What manners! . . . And to think Livia sold herself to that Shylock's son! . . . Ah, there's poor old D'Azollo!
> [*Goes over to the window-seat and interrupts the discussion by a romantic call*]
Rinaldo!

DUKE D'AZOLLO [*Rising and bowing vaguely*]
Signora! Neither of us is named Rinaldo.

ESTER DA GRASSO [*Piqued*]
You've forgotten Armida!

DUKE D'AZOLLO [*Puzzled*]
Armida?
> [*With exaggerated and mendacious romanticism*]
How could I forget Armida?

ESTER DA GRASSO [*Drawing him away*]
They warned me you and Fiuma had no eyes now but
for the Queen.

DUKE D'AZOLLO
But I do remember you!
    [*Sniffing her obviously strong scent*]
It's like a whiff of old times!

ESTER DA GRASSO
Ah, Rinaldo, those days on the yacht——

DUKE D'AZOLLO
You were on the yacht?
    [*Sniffs again*]
Ah, of course, I remember! Little Ester—with the
opera-singers——!

ESTER DA GRASSO [*Perceiving her husband is
    coming up*]
Hush! My husband!

DUKE D'AZOLLO
But he's deaf!

ESTER DA GRASSO
That was my previous husband.

DUKE D'AZOLLO
Santa Maria! My memory!

ESTER DA GRASSO
When I was whisked into exile among our obstreperous
peasant, I thought I'd go out of my mind. But I see
I've gone out of yours.

56

[*The door opens. A sudden hush falls on the
company. Those who are sitting, rise.* OMAR
appears.]

CAZOTTI [*Quietly to* RIFFONI]
Get up! And remember . . . !

RIFFONI [*Rising sullenly*]
For Salaret's sake.

OMAR
Her Exalted Majesty, the Queen.
[MARGHERITA *enters, escorted by the* BARON *and*
BARONESS LIVIA, *and accompanied by the* MARQUIS
FIUMA, *whose manly beauty is enhanced by a
chivalrous and devoted bearing, the* COUNTESS
CAZOTTI, *a dyed and bediamonded beauty, desperately young, and a pretty Maid of Honour.*
MARGHERITA, *though in the prime of youth and
beauty, wears an air of noble sadness.* HER
*costume is plain, with a pearl necklace, and she
enters unassumingly, not breaking off her conversation.* ALL *bow or curtsey, except* RIFFONI, *who has
folded his arms again. But the accidental group-
ing of the company, all clustering round the* QUEEN
*and hanging on her lips, assists the wilful posture
of* MOLP *to hide the rebel from the royal eyes.*]

THE QUEEN [*Smilingly, yet mechanically acknowl-
edging the greetings*]
But you have a wonderful house, Baron. That quaint
stone staircase from the courtyard!

57

BARON GRIPSTEIN
My Sigismondo says it dates from the Crusades, and
that those Byzantine reliefs in the hall were inserted
in the thirteenth century by the Duke of Dalmatia
during his happily brief conquest of our country. I
have had to cut his banqueting hall in twain—it was
too large for our humble selves.

QUEEN
What a pity! And how is dear Sigismondo?

LIVIA
He felt his presence would damp our spirits—he begs
Your Majesty to excuse him.

QUEEN
Oh, but that is morbid. Bring him down before I
go—don't forget. . . . Ah, there is my Rolmenian
friend!
    [SHE *extends her hand enthusiastically to the
    Rolmenian Minister, who kisses it*]
And how goes it with your beautiful country?

ROLMENIAN MINISTER
Alas, Madam, our army is undermined by Socialism.
    [CAZOTTI *and* ROXO *look at each other.*]

CAZOTTI [*Murmuring*]
Liar!

QUEEN
But I was just reading Prince Igmor's speech, congratulating the army on its morale.

ROLMENIAN MINISTER
That was for his royal father's consumption, Madam.
Since His Majesty's last stroke we dare not tell him
the truth.

QUEEN
I'm afraid it does not require strokes for sovereigns to
be kept in the dark, eh, Cazotti?
     [*Offers her hand smilingly.*]

CAZOTTI [*Bowing to kiss it*]
Your Majesty's intuitions are only too illuminating.

COUNTESS CAZOTTI
But it's quite true, Alexis. You don't even tell *me!*
     [*Laughter.*]

QUEEN [*Espying the* PRINCESS]
Ah, Princess, glad to see you in Valdania. How are
things in Bosnavina?—— But I forget, you come
from Carlsbad. I hope you left your rheumatism
there. That's where *you* ought to go, Marshal Roxo.

ROXO [*Kissing her hand*]
Ah, Madam, there is no cure for age and loneliness.

QUEEN
Poor Roxo! We are a pair.

ROXO
You, Madam, with your youth?
59

QUEEN

I am not so young as our friend, D'Azollo.

[SHE *turns to him and gives him her hand to kiss*]
The Duchess is not with you?

DUKE D'AZOLLO

If she were, would I look so young?
[*Laughter.*]

COUNTESS CAZOTTI

Oh, the monsters! This is what they say behind our
backs.
[*Laughter.*]

DUKE D'AZOLLO

But it was a compliment to the Duchess! She asks
me to convey her homage and regrets her headache
is too bad.

QUEEN

Too bad indeed! Since she resigned her Court duties,
she has never come to see me. And I particularly
wanted to see her to-night.

BARON GRIPSTEIN

She did hold out the hope of coming to the reception
. . . Shall I telephone Your Majesty's wishes?

QUEEN

Wouldn't her husband's telephoning have more in-
fluence?

60

DUKE D'AZOLLO [*Laughingly*]
I shall 'phone her we are thirteen at table.
> [*The* BARON *opens the door* R. *as if to conduct him*]

Don't trouble, Baron. I know where the telephone is.

LIVIA [*Smiling*]
And he complains of his memory!
> [*The* DUKE *totters out and the* BARON *closes the door.*]

BARON GRIPSTEIN
I trust Your Majesty will not wait for the Duchess——

QUEEN [*Smiling*]
Your *chef* need not be alarmed. Seriously, my dear Baron, the absence of this guest is not so annoying as the presence of others.

BARON GRIPSTEIN [*Turning pale*]
But the list was submitted——

QUEEN
Those skeletons at the feast, I mean.
> [*Looks towards* MOLP *and* RIFFONI, *the latter of whom, gazing at her dumbly as if spell-bound, has finally attracted her attention*]

You know how tired I am of seeing Molp, and now you had added a new protector, not even camouflaging him as a guest.

BARON GRIPSTEIN [*Miserably*]
I—I—believe me, Your Majesty, it was necessary.

61

QUEEN

In a private house? Though I was surprised to find my coming to you had leaked out, I encountered nothing but loyal demonstrations. True, in the Piazza de Pietra a woman sprang forward, and our brave Marquis turned pale. But she was only holding out a child to be touched against the evil eye.

CAZOTTI

There is always an evil eye on rulers, however popular.

BARON GRIPSTEIN

A man to whom a great treasure is entrusted cannot be too careful.

QUEEN

I appreciate your solicitude, but it spoils my appetite. Please send them away.

BARON GRIPSTEIN [*In agonised embarrassment*]

Certainly, Your Majesty. I had no idea of having them in the dining-room.

QUEEN

But I don't want them in the house at all.

BARON GRIPSTEIN

They shall not be.

QUEEN

But let them go at once.

62

BARON GRIPSTEIN
Of course.   Colonel Molp, you heard Her Majesty's
command.
   [MOLP *hesitates, embarrassed.*]

QUEEN
Don't look so sullen, Molp.   You know how much I
appreciate your devotion.   How is my little god-
child?

MOLP [*Brightening*]
Nina has cut another tooth, Your Majesty.

QUEEN
Dear little thing.   It must be very difficult for you
now your poor wife is dead.

MOLP
My mother has been with us: unfortunately, Your
Majesty, she has had to go home to my aged father—
a day distant.

QUEEN
Time *you* went home to say good-night to little Nina.

MOLP
Yes, Your Majesty.
   [*To* RIFFONI]
After you, my friend.
   [RIFFONI *does not move.*]

QUEEN
Why doesn't the man go?   Is he deaf?
63

CAZOTTI [*Audaciously*]
I suppose he was selected so as not to overhear our conversation.

QUEEN
But he looks so intelligent—he ought to be doing higher work.

ROXO
What can be higher than protecting Your Majesty?

BRIO [*Opening doors*]
Her Majesty is served.
[*There is a fresh view of the rose-crowned table and the gorgeous lackeys.*]

BARON GRIPSTEIN
Ouf!
[*Wipes his brow*]
Your Majesty, may I have the distinguished honour . . . ?
[*The* QUEEN *takes his arm, the other guests pair off consulting their slips; the* PRINCESS GONDAROFF *with the* ROLMENIAN MINISTER, *the* VISCOUNTESS PALESTRA *with the* PRINCE, *the* COUNTESS VILLOP *with the* MARQUIS FIUMA, *the* COUNTESS CAZOTTI *with the* VISCOUNT PALESTRA, SIGNORA DA GRASSO *with* CAZOTTI, *and the* MAID OF HONOUR *with* SIGNOR DA GRASSO.]

64

COUNTESS CAZOTTI [*Pushing past the* COUNTESS
    VILLOP]
Excuse me—I think we go first.
> [*The procession begins to move in, chattering and
> talking.*]

LIVIA [*To* MARSHAL ROXO]
Those telephone clerks! I'm afraid you'll have to
give *me* the wrong arm.
> [SHE *smilingly takes his left arm and brings up the
> rear.* BRIO *closes the folding doors behind her.
> Immediately through side-door* R., *as by secret
> instruction,* MOLP'S *men pour in, while from door*
> L., OMAR *and footmen and gendarmes enter.*]

MOLP
Now, Signor!

RIFFONI [*Turning on him and the newcomers with
    all the fury of long-suppressed speech*]
Minions, lackeys, lickspittles! Legions that could
dictate to those gorging despots and that insolent
minx——!

MOLP
Are you going quietly?

RIFFONI
More quietly than I shall return. By heaven and
hell and all your sluggard saints, this society you grovel
before shall feel my broom to the last cobweb!
65

A FOOTMAN [*Grinning*]
He's already been in the cellar.
    [*Laughter.*]

RIFFONI [*To* MOLP]
Not speak? The day shall come when she shall beg
for a word with me.
    [HE *shakes his fist towards the folding doors*]
A rivederla, Margherita!
    [COLONEL MOLP *steps towards him.*]

CURTAIN.

MOLP [*Now among the Guards, but somewhat dis-
    guised by a great scar on his cheek*]
Nor too much in the larder.

VANNI
Peace, you White swine. You get more grub than our
Dukes and Marquises in their skulking-holes. You're
a counter-revolutionary, that's what you are, a lousy
capitalist conspirator—strikes me I've seen your face
over a white shirt—Melano, did you say your name
was?

MOLP
A white shirt doesn't make a White. All I want is to
get to the front like those lucky beggars down there.

VANNI
All you want is to get two square meals a day.
    [*Laughter of the* GUARDS.]

MOLP
More food would be welcome, I don't deny. But I was
an officer before the Revolution and I——

VANNI
Officer or organ-grinder, we're all equal now and you're
under me—don't you forget it!

MOLP
But I'm wasted here!

VANNI
Wasted? Guarding the People's Hall? You look out,
Comrade, or my sister Fenella'll get her knife into you.

69

MOLP [*Wincing as at a memory, but recovering himself*]
Because I want to get *my* knife into the dirty Rolmenians?

VANNI
There's dirtier than the Rolmenians. How about your old Roxo?

MOLP
What about the Marshal?

VANNI
He's joined the Rolmenians, haven't you heard? Doesn't care a damn about us so long as he can restore the Queen to that chair there. I expect he'll guide Prince Igmor over our marshes. But they're no match for Riffoni, either of them, the saints be thanked.

MOLP
Not so certain. Riffoni after all is an amateur. Igmor has long led the Rolmenian forces and Roxo is a thundering tactician.

VANNI
Pooh! Pooh! The Marshal was never a patch on poor Marrobio. And now he's too shaky and rheumatic to cope with the President.

MOLP
But Igmor is young—and has already driven us out of Bosnavina.

70

VANNI
Hold your tongue, you pro-Rolmenian Royalist. You'll
never see the Queen squatting here again—if she's
alive at all!
[*There is a stir to the right*]
Attention!
[*The rank stiffens in rigid awe. Enter between the
pillars* RIFFONI *in a General's uniform. He looks
considerably aged, with a set and anxious coun-
tenance. The* GUARDS *present arms.* HE *seats
himself on the throne and examines papers for a
moment amid the severe silence.*]

RIFFONI [*Grasping a document*]
Comrade Vanni!

VANNI
Yes, my General.

RIFFONI
I see that Signor Oroscobonetti, the editor of the *Sera*,
was to be shot this morning. Has it been done?

VANNI
At dawn, my General.

RIFFONI
Good! The sun rose on one reactionary the less. How
did he die?

VANNI
Crying "Long live Liberty!"
71

RIFFONI
Liberty—to destroy the Workers' Republic! Ah, these bourgeois with their egoistic ideals.

VANNI
And may we read the *Sera* now?

RIFFONI [*Smiting the table*]
Corpo di Bacco! Surely you know that its printing press still eludes us. If you are found with anything except the State organs, the *Red Worker* and the *International Republican,* you'll get very short shrift, my friend.

VANNI [*With chattering teeth*]
Yes, my General. I wasn't asking for myself—but I've got a White among my own men.

RIFFONI [*Spasmodically grasping the pistol*]
A Judas among my bodyguard!

VANNI
He even admires Roxo!

RIFFONI [*Springing up*]
Who is this whited sepulchre?

VANNI
He was only sent me this morning, but it didn't take me long to nose him out. Stand forward, Melano.
[MOLP *obeys and salutes.*]

MOLP
I'm neither White nor Red. I'm a soldier.

72

RIFFONI
Your name, Comrade.

MOLP
Melano.

RIFFONI
So I just heard.   But I want your real name . . .
    [*A silence*]
Try to remember it!

MOLP
One can't forget one's name.

RIFFONI
I forgot mine when I sneaked back into Valdenia.
Come, come—your face haunts me . . . You know
we have instruments for making the dumb speak. What
were you before the Social Revolution?

MOLP [*Hesitates*]
I told you—a soldier.

VANNI
An officer, he told me, and he wants to go to the front.

RIFFONI
An officer, were you? What grade?

MOLP
Colonel.

RIFFONI
Ah, Colonel *Molp!* Of course, of course.   That new

scar of yours put me off. Then this time last year—
ha! ha! ha!

[*Relapses complacently on his throne*]

Where did you get that scar?

MOLP
In the attack on this Palace.

RIFFONI
You mean in the defence—you defended the miserable
Margherita.

MOLP
Could I desert her like Vanni?

VANNI
Could I desert the rest of the army—especially when
my sister Fenella———?

RIFFONI
Silence!

MOLP
It was that virago that jabbed my cheek when I was
trying to save the Marquis Fiuma———

RIFFONI
Who had already contrived the Queen's escape, the
devil take him.

MOLP [*Bowing his head*]
I hope he is with the angels. A gallant gentleman,
who loved the Queen.

74

RIFFONI
Yes, I dare say you do too. Ah, she has you all in her
net. She tried her tricks even on me, do you remember,
though she thought I was only one of your men.

MOLP
She only said you ought to be doing better work.

RIFFONI [*Smiling*]
She doesn't lack intelligence, the minx.

MOLP
And I didn't lack courtesy. I treated you like a
gentleman, though you treated me like a dog. When
I escorted you across the frontier, I offered to share
my sandwiches with you. Don't you remember?

RIFFONI
Perfectly. And though I refused your communistic
offer, I said it was an augury of the future—do you
remember that? Ah, you laughed then—you thought
me done with. Despite all your gangs of spies and
denouncers and *agents provocateurs,* you never tracked
the underground railway by which I was to creep back
when our propaganda had prepared the Revolution.

MOLP
It wasn't your propaganda—it was Rolmenia coming
to liberate Bosnavina from our yoke.

RIFFONI
Ah, but why did Rolmenia dare the adventure?
75

MOLP

Because Marrobio was no longer alive to frighten her.

RIFFONI

Marrobio's assassination was only a minor factor.
Rolmenia's real motive was to keep down the Socialism
in her army. She had to give it work and glory to
divert it. As a result—mark the irony of fate—she
exploded the Socialism in *our* army, which refused to
go to the shambles to keep a sister-country in subjec-
tion.

MOLP

But it *is* going—you have just sent it off!

RIFFONI

In self-defence, not aggression. Rolmenia hasn't understood that our Republic was quite content to lose
Bosnavina, that we should in any case have given back
the freedom violated by our rapacious Queen. Drunk
with success, the Rolmenians have dared to invade our
own sacred soil.

MOLP

I know, curse them. That's why I want to go to the
front.

RIFFONI [*Sardonically*]

I dare say. Anything sooner than the gallows, eh?
So, Colonel Molp, you thought to treat me as the
Bosnavian student treated Marrobio.

MOLP

By God, it is false!

76

RIFFONI

Obsolete oaths won't mend your case.

MOLP

But I was assigned here by the local Enrolment and
Distribution Committee appointed by the Industrial
Alliance under the Commissariat of Labour. In vain
I reminded them of the German proverb not to use
the piano for firewood. They pointed out it was a
rise on my last job.

RIFFONI

What was that?

MOLP [*In a low shamed voice*]

Cleaning out slaughter-houses and latrines—it was
when the typhus was raging.

RIFFONI

You explained to them you were *Colonel* Mop?

MOLP

Yes—er—that is, Colonel Melano.

RIFFONI

Why did you take a false name if not for false pur-
poses? So many old officers applied for jobs under
my Government and have found good ones too.

MOLP

Yes, but none had had my unpleasant relation with
you. I was afraid of your vengeance—rightly so, as
it has proved.

77

RIFFONI [*Bridling*]
How proved? You're not hanged yet, and if you are, it will be not by me but the Counter-Revolutionary Commission . . . If you were so frightened of me, why didn't you flee the country?

MOLP
I had my little girl—I couldn't leave her.

RIFFONI
And yet you want to go to the front!
    [*Laughter of the* GUARDS.]

VANNI
That little girl is a whopper.
    [*Laughter of the* GUARDS.]

RIFFONI
Silence, Comrades! I know there *was* a little girl. Called Nina, wasn't she?

MOLP
You know her name?

RIFFONI
Aha! . . . She is dead now, I suppose.

MOLP [*With a convulsive start*]
God forbid! She's with her grandmother in the country.

RIFFONI
So you *could* part with her.

MOLP
Because there is corn and milk in the village—it is so
far from towns.

RIFFONI ·
That is no answer. Town children are fed equally,
however we grown-ups may go short.

MOLP
But I assure you——

RIFFONI
It is Salaret's proudest achievement. Ah, Colonel, it
was when I saw *his* children starving under the pitiless
economic process that I vowed no child in our State
could ever go hungry or acold.

MOLP
But Nina——

RIFFONI
Fed, warmed, educated, entertained, cherished as never
before in human history, our children show such rosy
faces that one might say the Red Flag rides trimphant
in their cheeks.

MOLP [*Grimly*]
My Nina was white with hunger.

RIFFONI [*Agitated*]
Puns are out of place, Colonel . . . Vanni, did you
ever hear of children starving?

79

VANNI
I did hear something once, but as the gallows took the grumbler, I thought it was just White propaganda.

RIFFONI
The gallows shall take the Children's Committee, if this prove true, Colonel Molp. Fortunately Salaret will be back from his provincial tour this very morning —he shall at once investigate your Nina's case. But to come back to my question, you say you couldn't bear to leave her, yet you want to go to the front—whence you may never come back to her.

MOLP [*Struggling with his emotion*]
God help me! But can I see our country overrun by Rolmenians?

RIFFONI
They won't get far, I assure you. Why not stay here and go on with your old job?

MOLP [*Dazed*]
Go on with my old job?

RIFFONI [*Smiling*]
With me substituted for Margherita of course . . . You said you were not a White but a soldier. Your job with the Queen has lapsed. You don't feel bound to her any longer, I assume.

MOLP [*Slowly*]
No, I suppose I don't.

80

RIFFONI

Then take over *my* protection. I work in this room because thus I have under my eye the Piazza, which is the natural focus of revolution, and I sit in this chair because so I cannot well be stabbed in the back. But assassination hangs over it as that old sword of Alpastroom used to do. And why? Because I have made it for the first time the throne of justice . . . Come, why do you hesitate?

MOLP

I don't see how Nina could have got here without a God.

RIFFONI

What can you mean? What has that to do with it?

MOLP

The officers who took Government service told me they had to profess atheism.

RIFFONI

Humph! . . . But we can consider this a private post, not Government service.

MOLP

It is a heavy responsibility. I should have to take preventive measures——

RIFFONI

Who objects to that?

81

MOLP
You did, in the case of the Queen. You see they involve spies, even *agents provocateurs*——

RIFFONI
The Queen's life concerned only herself. Mine concerns the new social order. It is *that* they wish to assassinate—we cannot be squeamish with assassins. No, no, you do exactly as before. So that's settled . . .
    [*Begins writing*]
And whatever your salary was——

MOLP
Then you do permit differences of income?

RIFFONI
It is not strict Socialism, I know. But Salaret condones transitional measures.
    [*Gives him the paper he has written*]
There, Comrade Molp! Present this at the State Workers' Bureau, Section 17B, and they will give you a Colonel's uniform. And come back at noon to lunch with me—share my sandwiches!

MOLP
Thank you, my General—Comrade!

RIFFONI
And bring back little Nina to share yours.

MOLP [*Going*]
God bless you!

RIFFONI
Tut! Tut! If I permit you your superstition, do not
obtrude it.
[*A confused clamour penetrates from the Piazza*]
What is that? Stop, Molp! You may have to begin
your new functions at once. See what's going on.
[MOLP *opens the casement near the pillars and
steps out to survey the Piazza. The clamour clar-
ifies itself into cheers.* HE *comes in, closing the
window.*]

MOLP
It is Salaret coming back.

RIFFONI [*Relieved*]
Bravo!

MOLP
A man was throwing a bouquet into the car.

RIFFONI
Ah, we are still popular. *Viva* Salaret. Shout, Comrades!

GUARDS
Viva Salaret! *Evoè* Salaret!
[MOLP *goes out between the pillars with a military
salute which only* RIFFONI *returns.*]

RIFFONI
Why didn't you salute him? He is your officer now.

VANNI
A thousand apologies, my General.
83

RIFFONI
And don't forget to salute Comrade Salaret, though
he is not a soldier.

VANNI
Do you hear, pigs—Comrades?

RIFFONI
And remind me to speak to him about Comrade Molp's
little girl.

VANNI
Yes, my General.

RIFFONI
I can't understand, Comrade, why you didn't report
to me those rumours of hungry children. Are there
any other grievances you know of? Tell me, Comrade.

VANNI
Well, Comrade, it doesn't seem right I shouldn't get
more rations than my men.

RIFFONI [*Winningly*]
But that *is* Communism, Comrade. Under the old
system some people got too much and some too little.

VANNI
Now we all get too little.

RIFFONI [*Rather irritated*]
That's only temporary. Wait till Rolmenia gives us
breathing-space to organize production.

84

VANNI
But if it's the dictation of the proletariat, why can't
we dictate ourselves more rations all round?

RIFFONI
That is silly.

VANNI
But my brother-in-law, the brooch-maker, says——

RIFFONI [*Sharply*]
The brooch-maker! Does he still make brooches?

VANNI [*Alarmed*]
With your head, my President.

RIFFONI
Let him look to his own! Brooches indeed, when we
want every possible hand for earth-labour, clothing
or poison gas. How came the Enrolment and Distribution Committee to allow it?

VANNI
He—he is Chairman of the Committee, my General.

RIFFONI
The Burial Committee will soon be busy with him.
   [*Writes.*]

VANNI [*Panic-stricken*]
But my poor sister, Fenella——!

RIFFONI
Silence! The Republic has no use for slackers and
85

shirkers. I expected you to ask for the privilege of arresting him.

VANNI [*Cringing*]
So I would if it wasn't for Fenella. He's a cocky little brute, is Stefano, and when he was made Chairman two chairs wouldn't hold him. But remember how Fenella that night—how she helped to make the Republic.

RIFFONI
Is that a reason her husband should help to destroy it?
    [*Enter between the pillars* PROFESSOR SALARET, *carrying a bouquet. The* GUARDS *salute.* SALARET *is a prophetic-bearded, elderly figure, but looks tired and heavy-eyed beyond his years.* RIFFONI *springs up and hurries down the dais to salute him on both cheeks.*]

RIFFONI
Welcome home, Master. Even more welcome than your reassuring telegrams.

SALARET [*Returning his kisses*]
So glad to find you in Scaletta. I was afraid——

VANNI [*Imploringly*]
My General——!

RIFFONI
Not another word. Every man who abuses his position must hang!
86

VANNI
But, Comrade, in the Bosnavian war——!

RIFFONI [*Handing him paper*]
Give Captain Lambri the order for his arrest, and
withdraw. March!
    [VANNI *motions miserably to his men to file out
    with him*]
Ah, Salaret, I cannot tell you what a comfort it has
been amid all the chaos to learn that the peasantry
was sound, that as far up the river as your yacht could
penetrate, the new brotherhood was working blissfully.

SALARET
It is impossible to imagine more enthusiastic activity
than I left behind me everywhere.

RIFFONI
Ah, Salaret, you are indeed fortunate. To how few
pioneers is it given to see their vision translated into
life! Surely you disprove the Roman proverb: Call
no man happy till he is dead.

SALARET [*Tugging at his beard*]
Humph! You realise, of course, that what enraptures
them is the possession of the land. While some had
seized it in advance, others did not even understand
it was to be theirs for nothing—they offered me money
to transmit to their refugee masters.

RIFFONI
Poor simple souls. But I hope you made it clear that

it really belongs to the State and that it was to be worked in common.

SALARET
I would not press that point overmuch now, Vittorio. One big step at a time. Get your factory-workers as contented as your land-workers and then we can move further.

RIFFONI
But the nationalisation of the industries obviously involves work in common. You can't give each man a machine!

SALARET
But you added to their discontent by denationalising what was already nationalised.

RIFFONI [*Fretfully*]
You mean religion. But we couldn't compromise in *everything*. How can a modern State be built on these grotesque beliefs?

SALARET
But was there any need to turn half the churches into cinemas?

RIFFONI [*Smiling*]
I doubled their congregations. The Entertainment Committee needed them to instil Socialism—the one true religion. Besides, you, yourself, transferred their ikons and Church plate to your Exchequer.

88

SALARET
The Church treasure couldn't be left in the cinemas.

RIFFONI
Don't let us argue to-day, dear Salaret. You must
be tired. Sit down.
    [*Drawing him towards the throne.*]

SALARET
No, no. Not there!

RIFFONI
It is there you should have been from the first.

SALARET
I know my place better. I am—our conversation has
proved it once again—a mere curb on your creative
vehemence. As Finance Minister I dock your schemes,
as Commissary of the Interior I mutilate them to
correspond with the possible.

RIFFONI
But it was your books that inspired everything!

SALARET
Was it I that lit the spark that glorious night? No,
no. To hold the masses, to breathe fire into the army,
to repress revolution—that needs you. Ah, trust the
people to know its true leader.
    [*Presses him into the throne, places the bouquet on
    the table, and sits beside him*]
Why do you smile?
89

RIFFONI
Not at your exaggerations. I was remembering how
I told the Duke D'Azollo I would come back on his
steam-yacht, with the Red Flag flying. And if I didn't
fulfil my prophecy literally, my sending you on the
yacht to supervise land-distribution came very near.
You really found it better than your limousine?

SALARET
Incomparably. You see one wasn't dependent on
wretched country hotels or village inns—one had a
floating home.

RIFFONI
I never thought of that . . . Ah, if the Duke had
only employed it like you, instead of making it a floating
harem.

SALARET [*Hastily changing the conversation*]
I even ensured the draining of the marshes by dis-
tributing them too.

RIFFONI
Good! We sorely need more home-grown food.

SALARET
Oh, the marshes can merely make pasture-land.

RIFFONI
That's something. If only these cursed militarists had
conquered their own country!

SALARET [*With a grim smile*]
Isn't that what Roxo is trying to do now? Your radio
90

announcing the bad news quite spoilt my homecoming.
Indeed, I fully expected to find you away at the front.
You are not alarmed?

RIFFONI
On the contrary. Igmor's invasion has stopped the
factory strikes and pulled the country together—it may
be the saving of the Workers' Republic.

SALARET
How splendid! But all the same Prince Igmor——

RIFFONI
Trust General Hussein. He may not be as dashing as
poor Marrobio, but he's wilier.

SALARET
You comfort me. But fancy Roxo going over to the
enemy!

RIFFONI
I heard him once ask what could be higher than protecting the Queen. The old fanatic probably imagines
that once Margherita was restored, Prince Igmor
would trot home like a lamb. But of course he would
simply annex us.

SALARET
According to Armida——
  [*Tugs at his beard in confusion*]
I mean, they say it is Margherita that Igmor really
wants to annex—but perhaps that is all gossip.

RIFFONI [*Rising, agitated*]
It's all true—I found it in the archives. And she was
ready to prostitute herself to that pig-eyed princeling,
if only he would help her to conquer Bosnavina.
  [*Grimly*]
But Igmor will neither annex Margherita nor Valdania. He will be lucky even to get home.

SALARET
You seem very sure.

RIFFONI [*Laying his hand on Salaret's shoulder*]
Be proud of your son, Salaret. The experiments have
succeeded at last.

SALARET
Guido's aerial torpedoes?

RIFFONI
Kites we now call them for short. Yes, charged with
his new poison gas, they annihilate in their descent all
life—for at least a square kilometre.

SALARET
How horrible!

RIFFONI
Not so horrible as the annihilation of the Workers'
Republic—the spiritual hope of the world. It was to
organise this last line of defence that I flew back here
yesterday—unfortunately the Kites are ponderous and
we lack transport to convey them to the front. Igmor
must come here if he wants to be wiped out . . .
Would I could wipe out our deficit as easily!

SALARET
The Church treasure was a great disappointment. The jewels in the ikons had already been stolen by the priests.

RIFFONI
I know. I am not criticising your balance-sheet. But if only Gripstein had not been so obstinately Royalist —by the way, thanks to the patriotic wave caused by the Rolmenian advance, he was betrayed into our hands yesterday.

SALARET
Bravo! Then can't you convert him?

RIFFONI
To Socialism? More easily to Judaism!

SALARET [*Smoothing his beard*]
Ha! ha! ha!

RIFFONI
He won't give away the hiding place of the Queen, or of the printing-press of the *Sera,* though I am sure he knows both. Apropos, Oroscobonetti was shot this morning.

SALARET [*Starting up*]
My dear Vittorio! Not so many executions.

RIFFONI
He was more dangerous to the Republic than Prince Igmor.

93

SALARET
But I thought you had stopped his paper.

RIFFONI
It still appears—in the most unexpected places.
Exploiting our every error and drawback. Wittily—
I trace the Duke's pen. Ah, there is the latest copy.
    [*Picks it up from litter on table.*]

SALARET [*Taking it*]
"Shorter Working Hours Demanded — An Eight
Hour Day for the Hangman." There! Just what I
was saying. The first moment I came in, you were
talking of hanging somebody. Armida—er—a lady
told me you've been nicknamed "Riffoni the Red."

RIFFONI
Of course I'm a Red. But do you know what they
call you? "Salaret the Soft!" Alliteration always
pleases the people. But you won't get far with softness, believe me, dear Master. We tried that years
enough, you and I. We wore out our quills and our
throats. Ah, it is unimaginable how greedy, lazy and
ungrateful men are, how cunning and evasive. Three
times have I closed and sealed up the old markets, yet
illicit buying and selling continues, and thieves and
speculators plunge their dirty paws into the State
stores. In vain I raid the houses in the middle of the
night to search for army necessities, my very detectives
spirit them away. I tell you, Salaret, terror is the only
shaping-tool. The Earthly Paradise we plan must be
cleared of weeds: pitilessly—for pity's own sake.

94

VANNI [*Reappearing timidly between the pillars*]
My General, you asked me——

RIFFONI
I asked you to give Captain Lambri the order for his
arrest.

VANNI
But the little Nina——!

RIFFONI
Oh, that!
    [VANNI *salutes and begins to retire*]
There's a case in point. Children unfed by some mis-
management or misappropriation. You must look
into it . . . Wait a moment, Corporal. Fetch me
Comrade Gripstein.

VANNI
Yes, my General.

RIFFONI
And on second thoughts collect Comrade Livia, too.
. . . No, let one of your men get the lady—we don't
want the two prisoners consulting.

VANNI
I understand, Comrade.
    [*Exit.*]

SALARET
What are you going to do?

RIFFONI
Try my shaping-tool.

SALARET
More terrorism?

RIFFONI
The Baron must be frightened into confessing where
he has concealed his gold reserve. And his daughter-
in-law, who was a maid of honour, surely knows where
the Queen is burrowing.

SALARET
Why not let lost monarchs lie?

RIFFONI
As long as she lives, she will be the storm-centre of
reaction. You yourself said her beauty was the real
cause of Igmor's invading us. Even the currency you
have failed to stamp out is infectious. Every coin
with her image is a counter-revolutionary.
    [*Produces one*]
Look at the hussy! She will always have a train of
young monarchists all in love with her.

SALARET
Bah! *Cazotti* uncaught is more formidable.

RIFFONI
More sinister and spidery, but not more dangerous—
unless you mean he has his wife's death to revenge.

SALARET
To revenge?
    [*Laughs mirthlessly*]
From all I hear the shot that killed the Countess

removed the one clog on his career. The woman simply dragged him down.

RIFFONI
All women drag one down.

SALARET
You haven't much experience.

RIFFONI
I had my youthful plunge—thanks to too much pocket-money. Ah, how good it was to come up to the surface and breathe the clean sweet air of service! It was your books dragged me up from the slime.

SALARET [*With uneasy facetiousness*]
And yet people call them dry. Odd that your father's books bored you then. But it's a wise child that knows his own father.
    [*Moves towards the curtains*]
I suppose my old rooms——

RIFFONI
Yes, the Queen's suite is still at your disposal—I stick to my camp-bed in the basement. But you will surely wait to tackle Gripstein?

SALARET
No, thanks. I don't like experiments in terror.

RIFFONI
But as Finance Minister you are peculiarly interested.
97

SALARET [*Drawing aside curtains and revealing* OMAR *on duty with a pistol in his girdle*]
I would rather have a wash . . . Well, Omar, how are you?

OMAR [*Salaams*]
Great is the mercy of Allah.
[HE *closes the curtains behind himself and* SALARET. *Enter through the pillars* BARON GRIPSTEIN *followed by* CORPORAL VANNI. *The* BARON *looks wistful, unkempt, unbrushed and woe-begone.*]

RIFFONI
Ah, Comrade Gripstein, good-morning.
[BARON *does not reply*]
So you are still tongue-tied?

BARON GRIPSTEIN
I have nothing to say.

RIFFONI
And if we try some of those quaint instruments we unearthed in the vault—the prickly hare, the mouth-widener——?

BARON GRIPSTEIN
You will not.

RIFFONI
And why not, pray?

BARON GRIPSTEIN
You founded a Society for the Prevention of Cruelty——

98

RIFFONI
Surgery is not cruelty.   An operation for dumbness——

BARON GRIPSTEIN
Must be done under chloroform.

RIFFONI
Bah!   Your fencing will not save you . . . Nor your
daughter-in-law, either.
> [LIVIA, *as he speaks, is brought in through the
> curtains, pale, but in better fettle.* SHE *smiles at
> the* BARON *and they look lovingly at each other*]
Give Comrade Livia a chair.

LIVIA
I would rather stand.

RIFFONI
As you please.   Don't imagine your disdain impresses
me, any more than it did in your own salon.   Why
you should be so proud of never having earned your
clothes and keep, your God alone knows.   And you
weren't too proud to blend your blood with the breed
of Shylock! . . .
> [LIVIA *winces*]
Come now, my patience is at an end.   Where is the
Queen?

LIVIA
Why not consult the *Sera?*

RIFFONI
You are adding insolence to your iniquities.   Where
is the Queen?

99

LIVIA
With the Duke and Duchess D'Azollo.

RIFFONI
Yes, and the Duke and Duchess with the Queen. Do not try me too far.
[*Turns again to* GRIPSTEIN]
Where is your bank bullion?

BARON GRIPSTEIN
A Socialist State does not need gold.

RIFFONI
It must pay for its imports.

BARON GRIPSTEIN
And thus foster Capitalism abroad?

RIFFONI
It is not our fault if Socialism is not everywhere simultaneous.

BARON GRIPSTEIN
And since it can never be simultaneous it can never *be*.

RIFFONI
The sunrise is not simultaneous but the world rolls always towards it. Where is your gold, I say? . . . Ah, the old British King would have taken out your teeth.

BARON GRIPSTEIN
You will find only a little gold there.

100

LIVIA
Ha! ha! ha!

RIFFONI
Silence, woman. And you, Jew, understand that by
the law of Valdania all bank-assets must be nationalised.

BARON GRIPSTEIN
So must all raw stuffs: yet to keep your factories
going you yourselves buy secretly of speculators and
profiteers.

RIFFONI
We are above the law: you are under it. What have
you done with your bullion?

BARON GRIPSTEIN [*Sullenly*]
Marshal Roxo has it.

RIFFONI
You traitor! Then he has carried it to Rolmenia!

BARON GRIPSTEIN [*Jubilant*]
Has he? Then Margherita will be restored!

RIFFONI [*Grimly*]
You shall not live to see it.

BARON GRIPSTEIN
I died when Sigismondo died. Ah, the poor blind boy
could not see his murderers! But God saw them! I
will repay, saith the Lord, I will repay.

RIFFONI
Ha! ha! ha! Let Him first pay what He owes the old
régime. Corporal Vanni!

VANNI
Yes, my General.

RIFFONI
String the Jew up at once.

BARON GRIPSTEIN [*Transformed from prophet
to poltroon*]
Not *hanged!* Creator of the Universe!

RIFFONI
What does it matter to one dead already?

LIVIA
You dare not hang a Knight of the Order of the
Redeemer.

RIFFONI
And who will redeem him? He doesn't deserve a
soldier's death . . . Now, Corporal!

BARON GRIPSTEIN
But give me time—an hour—half an hour——!

RIFFONI
What do you need time for?

BARON GRIPSTEIN
For prayer—repentance—the confession of my sins.

RIFFONI
Surely a week wouldn't suffice for your sins against
102

Labour. Give him ten minutes, Comrade, perhaps he
will repent of his refusal to help the Republic.

BARON GRIPSTEIN
God bless you. But I need a Rabbi.

LIVIA [*Revolted*]
A Rabbi? You!

BARON GRIPSTEIN [*Frenzied*]
A Rabbi, for God's sake! I have trespassed——!
    [*Begins to beat his breast and recite the Hebrew
    confession*]
Al chêt shechetanu lefanecha——

RIFFONI
Stop these mummeries. The State recognises no holy
slackers. They have all accepted useful work under
the Republic—the Patriarch, the Mufti, the Grand
Rabbi. Only the Cardinal has so far managed to
evade our Enrolment Committees—but we shall yet
harness him.

LIVIA
The Church has survived worse persecutions.

RIFFONI
Persecutions? Who interferes with your performances? We won't pay for them, that's all. Apropos,
since the Cardinal does no State work, let *him* be
fetched to the Baron.

BARON GRIPSTEIN
No! No! Not a priest! A Rabbi!

103

RIFFONI
You queer pious people—one man's saviour is another
man's Satan! Take him away! . . . Wait! Unless
within the ten minutes he reveals the Queen's hiding-
place, let his daughter-in-law dangle beside him.

LIVIA
Do not speak, father!

BARON GRIPSTEIN [*Huskily*]
You to be hanged!

LIVIA
What is death but stepping across a frontier—into
the arms of Christ!

BARON GRIPSTEIN
Ah, if I could believe in Him!

LIVIA
You do—you must. Pray to the Sacred Heart and
His Precious Blood. He will guide you to God.

BARON GRIPSTEIN [*Clutching at her hand*]
You must guide me—ah, I see only a black road.

LIVIA
Sigismondo is waiting to lend you his eyes——

BARON GRIPSTEIN
Out of my first earnings, we moved into a tiny two-
roomed house and there was gas. O the light and hope
104

when it first blazed yellow from our match! . . . And
that it should all have come to this!

> [*Covers his eyes.* MOLP, *now in a colonel's uniform,
> re-enters between the pillars.*]

RIFFONI
Ah, Colonel, the very man I wanted . . . How nicely
that fits you! . . . Your first job will, I hope, be as
amusing to you as it is to me. You are to conduct
these two undesirables across the frontier.

MOLP [*Surveying them*]
I see the joke.

BARON GRIPSTEIN [*Dazed*]
The frontier?

RIFFONI
Not the one with Christ in the custom-house . . .
Nor, Colonel, the Bosnavinian frontier where they
would only reinforce the other White refugees. Take
my motor-car. And divide your sandwiches with them
—ham, I hope.

BARON GRIPSTEIN
We are not to be hanged? O God of Israel!

LIVIA
O Blessed Mary!

RIFFONI
Settle between yourselves which has saved you. But I
will tell you, Baron, *what* has saved you—the anony-
mous pension you paid Salaret!

105

BARON GRIPSTEIN
You know?

RIFFONI [*Smiling*]
Haven't we got possession of all your papers of no
value? Ah, the agony when friend Molp was escorting *me* out of Valdania—the thought that I was leaving
Salaret and his little ones to starve. But those banknotes the post brought him every first of the month——
    [HIS *voice breaks down.* HE *extends his hand,*
    which the BARON *takes as in a dream*]
Addio. Don't counterplot too much.

BARON GRIPSTEIN [*Still dazed*]
How truly is it written that charity averts the evil
decree!

RIFFONI
Look after him, Baroness, he's a good old soul, despite all his religions.

LIVIA
I should have been more grateful, Signoir, had you
played with us less cruelly.

RIFFONI
I am sorry that it was necessary in the State interest
to try to extract the information. I have failed and
there's an end of it. As a matter of fact, I haven't
the power to send people to death without a trial.
Find them Austrian passports, Molp, else the Baron
will be refused admission as a Socialist. Ha! ha!
ha!

106

MOLP
Then you won't expect me to lunch.

RIFFONI
Ha! I'm sorry.   But come as soon as they are safe
and report——
    [*Re-enter* SALARET *through the curtains*]
Ah, Salaret, just in time to say good-bye to your
benefactor.

SALARET
He has disgorged the bullion?

RIFFONI
No, no—I was referring to the banknotes he sent you
every month.

SALARET
He? But *you* sent them!

RIFFONI
I? I could scarcely keep myself.   Didn't I tell you I
discovered they were his secret amends for having
sacked you?

SALARET
That was very kind of you, Baron.   But I had rather
you had given me back my editorship.

BARON GRIPSTEIN [*With a twinkle*]
You can have it back now, if you like.

RIFFONI
Ha! ha! ha!   The old chap has more humour than
his God.

107

SALARET
But I accept your offer. Where is the printing-office?

RIFFONI
Ha! ha! ha! Well countered, Salaret! Write him an order on the Treasury for his advances — with interest.

BARON GRIPSTEIN
No, not interest. Don't rob me of my good deed.

SALARET [*Writing*]
Very well.

BARON GRIPSTEIN
But you must double the principal.

SALARET
Eh?

BARON GRIPSTEIN
The currency has halved its value since you became Finance Minister.

LIVIA
How can you chaffer so, Baron? When we have just escaped death.

BARON GRIPSTEIN
That is why, *carissima*. We have to *live*. What with Bosnavina repudiating her loan, even the fare to America would be a consideration.

> [OMAR *comes through the curtains towards* RIF-FONI, *bearing a letter on a salver.*]

108

LIVIA [*Shocked*]
You here, Omar!

OMAR [*Apologetically*]
I had to live, your Excellencies.

BARON GRIPSTEIN
Just what I was saying, Omar.   And very glad to see
you alive.
[RIFFONI *takes the letter and begins opening it.*]

SALARET [*Simultaneously handing* GRIPSTEIN *the
order on the Treasury*]
There!   You can't say the Workers' Republic is as
repudiatory as Bosnavina.

RIFFONI [*Looking up*]
You'd better lend him *your* car to the frontier, Salaret
—it's more comfortable than mine.   Unless he'd like
my aeroplane.

BARON GRIPSTEIN [*Shuddering*]
God forbid!
[RIFFONI, *amused, begins to read the letter, and*
MOLP *speaks to* SALARET, *evidently about the
motor-car.*]

OMAR [*To* GRIPSTEIN]
Is Signor Brio alive, Effendi?

BARON GRIPSTEIN
My majordomo? . . . How should I know?
109

OMAR [*Lowering his voice*]
And Her Majesty?
[GRIPSTEIN *makes a warning gesture that* MOLP *is approaching.*]

MOLP
Are you ready, Baron?

BARON GRIPSTEIN
Perefctly. Signor Riffoni, as you have been merciful, may you find mercy. *Addio.*

RIFFONI [*Absently, absorbed in the letter*]
À rivederla.
[MOLP *salutes equally unmarked and together with* VANNI *and the* GUARD *escorts the* BARON *and* LIVIA *out.* RIFFONI *gives a long low whistle.*]

SALARET
What is it, Vittorio?

RIFFONI [*Joyously*]
The beginning of the end!
[HE *hands him the letter.* SALARET *tugs at his beard nervously.* RIFFONI'S *face falls at a sudden suspicion*]
But do you know if that is his handwriting? It may be an assassin.

SALARET
It may be worse—it may be the man himself. . . . What is the Signor like, Omar?

110

OMAR
Very shabby, Effendi. Like a deserter. I marvel
they let him cross to my side of the Palace. He must
know his way about it.

RIFFONI
He would.

OMAR
They say Captain Lambri let him in because he saw
him throw a bouquet into your car.

SALARET
The rogue! But is he fat, thin, long, short?

OMAR
Short and not so fat as last year.

RIFFONI
Ha! Then you know him.

OMAR
No, Effendi. But his garments hang loose.

SALARET
Quite a Sherlock Holmes.

RIFFONI
Who sees everything except the central fact. You
didn't recognise Cazotti?

OMAR
The Prime Minister! . . . The counter-revolutionist,
I mean. But Count Cazotti's face was hairless and
this man is bearded like a Medina pilgrim.

111

RIFFONI
Beards, unlike brains, can grow. Let him come. . . .
    [*Exit* OMAR]
Ah, I nearly cried "Thank God!"—such is the force
of early idioms. The Workers' Republic is safe!
Embrace me, Salaret.

SALARET [*Waving him off*]
Beware of Cazotti's embrace. The Republic safe,
forsooth! If you accept his offer to betray the Queen's
hiding-place, you will have to amnesty him — he is
even capable of demanding the reward for delivering
himself up! Once he has got his foot in again, he
will renew communication with Roxo, and the traitor
within will deliver the citadel to the traitor without.

RIFFONI
You overlook, dear Master, that once we capture the
Queen, there will be no dynasty for Roxo to restore.
    [CAZOTTI *comes through the curtains which are*
    parted by OMAR; *a broken refugee with a ragged*
    iron-grey beard and whiskers]
So, Cazotti, the game's up!

CAZOTTI
Yes, King Capital is dead, long live the Workers'
Republic!

RIFFONI [*Astonished*]
You're a Socialist now?

CAZOTTI
I always was.

112

SALARET
What!!

CAZOTTI
Every statesman is, seeing that the States is only a
Social group. Individualism is anarchy.

SALARET
Oh really! Do you take us for innocents?

CAZOTTI
Innocence and politics are incompatible. Your days
of innocence are over, Signor Salaret.

SALARET [*Sharply*]
I don't understand you.

CAZOTTI
May I sit down? I am tired.
    [HE *finds a chair and sits looking round*]
The room seems to have lost colour! Ah, you have
removed the window-Madonna!

RIFFONI
She let in the air through a hundred bullet-holes

CAZOTTI
Yes, and a bullet, on my poor wife, who had such a
foolish faith in her protection.
    [*Covers his eyes and is silent a space. Looks up
    fiercely*]
Ah, I daresay you think I am posing at bereavement.
My wife was often absurd, I know, but I can't forget
that with a dozen rich aspirants for her hand, she
113

married the struggling journalist when he hadn't a soldo.

[*Covers his eyes again.*]

SALARET [*Breaking the silence sardonically*]
So you always were a Socialist?

CAZOTTI [*Animated again*]
What was the constitution I gave Valdania if not Socialist?

SALARET
It was Democratic, not Socialist.

CAZOTTI
Your paper said the contrary.

SALARET [*Outraged*]
My paper?

CAZOTTI
Practically. You said that now every man had a vote, Labour being the overwhelming majority had only to return a Workers' Parliament to ensure the dictation of the proletariat.

RIFFONI
That was true in theory but in practice the propertied classes would have resisted expropriation with the knife.

CAZOTTI
I quite agree *they* would have become the revolutionary party. Anyhow, you don't suppose it was tenderness for *them* that instigated my reforms? Did
114

not the Duke D'Azollo complain I had commandeered his farm? The aristocratic party I overthrew used to fling at me that I had begun on a tub. In reality I began lower—on a doorstep. I am not only a son of the people, but a nameless son. Ah, it was not capital that rocked my cradle. Never have I lost the burning sympathy with my own class that springs from the sense of a wronged childhood.

RIFFONI
But you said in my own hearing that self-interest is the only practicable pivot of society—you quoted your dentist.

CAZOTTI [*Smiling*]
I thought you would throw that in my teeth.
    [RIFFONI *smiles*]
He has now charge of yours by the way, and your every smile shows the world he was wrong and that happily human nature is better than we thought. You have proved that love of the State is sufficient to make the wheels go round—I can hear them humming all around me.

RIFFONI [*With satisfaction*]
Ha!

SALARET
A quick conversion.

CAZOTTI
And if I had not been converted, what would you have said? That like the Bourbons I learn nothing

and forget nothing. I overrated the power of resistance of the possessing classes. All wars in my experience have been economic at bottom. What then, I thought, would be the bloodiness of the war which is economic at top too! Your colleague has just admitted he thought the propertied classes would have fought even constitutional expropriation to the death. Had I forseen how feeble would be their defence, or even with what comparative apathy the workers would submit to docketing and regimentation, I would have gone forward more boldly. You accused me of moving in spirals. It is true. As a workaday politician I did not believe the popular intelligence sufficiently advanced to follow a straight lead. I had not your genius and courage for a frontal attack on the old order. But if I moved spirally, the spirals were always upward, and now that I have made the last turn—here I am at your side!

RIFFONI [*Rather dazed*]
You offer co-operation as well as information?

CAZOTTI
In any capacity, however humble.

SALARET
After you expelled him from Valdania?

RIFFONI
Ah, I was forgetting. . . . And you, Comrade Cazotti, forget you are not now in the Chamber of Deputies. Here we demand Truth.

CAZOTTI

I expelled you from Valdania because I thought your frontal attacks would only stiffen the bourgeois against my spiral methods.

SALARET

But when we achieved your secret aim, why did you not join us at once, why lie low so long?

CAZOTTI

Were you in the mood to have me, or rather were your ferocious followers, the Fenellas and Lambris? I had to wait for the first ferment to be over.

SALARET

Or for the revolution to succeed.

RIFFONI

Or for the revolution to succeed. Then you throw us bouquets.

CAZOTTI

And do you call this success? Western Europe drawing daily further from you, and the Rolmenian army nearer? No, Comrades, what I offer to share is your risk, not your success. It is the ruin of my career if you are conquered.

RIFFONI

We shall not be conquered. At the worst our Kites——

SALARET

Sh! You are indiscreet. . . . And what help, Count Cazotti, can *you* bring us?

CAZOTTI
What help can *I* bring? Leaving out that I bring
you the Queen, cannot you see that with my European
reputation my accession to your ranks will show the
world that opposition is futile, that you are here to
stay?

RIFFONI
Ha!

CAZOTTI
While my personal relations with the various Cabinets
will ensure the recognition of the Republic. I can
pour oil on the troubled waters.

SALARET
Thank you—we can offer our own petroleum concessions.

RIFFONI
Ha! ha! ha!

CAZOTTI
The capitalist countries may deal with you, but they
will not recognize you politically.

RIFFONI
Just what we want. What you call our Fenellas and
Lambris would resent our recognizing *them*. You are
sure that if we deal with them, we can rely on their
not recognizing us officially?

CAZOTTI [*Smiling*]
Even for that you need a practised diplomatist. And
118

still more for the oil concessions will you need a practised Finance Minister.

SALARET [*Bounding*]
What!! . . . Vittorio, we must discuss this alone. . . . I insist.
[RIFFONI *strikes the gong on his table once.* VANNI *and his men file in.*]

RIFFONI
Remove Count Cazotti till I signal again.
[*They march him out.*]

CAZOTTI [*At exit*]
Like you, Comrade Riffoni, I shall return.

SALARET
O my guileless Vittorio, with all your genius! The scoundrel is playing on your nobility.

RIFFONI [*A little restive*]
Say gullibility and have done with it. Surely what he says is true—his accession will be the seal of our success. And he is devilishly able.

SALARET
Devilishly. A sinister spider, as you put it just before. Stamp upon him.

RIFFONI
And let the Queen escape?

SALARET
We shall find her without him.

119

RIFFONI
Not so sure.

SALARET
The new patriotic wave you tell me of will fling her at
our feet, as it flung Gripstein.

RIFFONI
And in the meantime her damnable face is to hover in
the air, obscuring our future.

SALARET
You exaggerate her importance.

RIFFONI
At any rate I cannot exaggerate Cazotti's. Surely the
Interior is burden enough for you. Suppose you hand
him over the Finances—he did do wonders with them.

SALARET
Under Gripstein's coaching. Even then look at the
debt he left us.

RIFFONI
That was the Bosnavinian war. As you wittily said
in the *Sera,* we died beyond our means.

SALARET
Yes, but who sent us to death? Cazotti.

RIFFONI
No, no, Margherita was the murderess. Margherita,
with her craving to add Bosnavina to her dominions
and Duchess to her title. Ah, Cazotti will more than

120

atone for his past, if he really delivers her into our
hands.

SALARET
Then let him deliver her—and let them die together!

RIFFONI [*Surprised and shocked*]
Salaret! How could we act so dishonourably? We
promised amnesty to any informant——

SALARET [*Tugging at his beard*]
Did we? Then Cazotti's information must be refused.

RIFFONI
Why? Amnesty does not imply accepting him as a
colleague, nor even perhaps keeping him in the country
—I could deport him. That would complete the turning of the tables. Ha! ha! ha! But we *must* have
the Queen!

SALARET
Vittorio, I beseech you.

RIFFONI [*Touched*]
A Salaret does not beseech. Let the dog go!
    [*Strikes gong.*]

SALARET
Unhanged?

RIFFONI
You said not so many hangings.

SALARET
One hanging may save many.

We can always catch him again — the brute is sadly winded.

[*Already* CAZOTTI *is returning with* VANNI *and the* GUARDS, *who range themselves against the wall.* RIFFONI *seats himself on the throne*]

Count Cazotti, Comrade Salaret and I have considered both your offer of information and your offer of co-operation, and in both cases——

[*Enter* OMAR *through the curtains*]

I didn't ring.

OMAR

No, Effendi, but the Commissary of Police is telephoning——

RIFFONI

Komak? Can't you take the message?

OMAR

He says it is too great for any ear but the President's.

RIFFONI

I shall really have to instal the receiver here. And then farewell even to the dregs of peace. Salaret, will you convy our decision to Count Cazotti?

SALARET

With pleasure. And give Komak my greetings. He was my boy's college-chum and subsidizer, you remember! A splendid fellow!

[RIFFONI *follows* OMAR *out.* SALARET *seats himself on the dais, but not on the throne*]

Count Cazotti, we have come to the conclusion that since leopards do not change their spots——

CAZOTTI [*Cooly*]
Hadn't you and I likewise better discuss this alone?

SALARET
There is nothing to discuss. And if there was, do you
suppose I would trust myself within reach of the
leopard's paw?

CAZOTTI
Very well. Do not blame me if my revelations before
the proletariat——
    [*Their eyes meet.*]

SALARET
Coporal Vanni, search this man for weapons.

VANNI
Yes, Excel—— Comrade!
    [*Taps* CAZOTTI *everywhere with his one arm*]
Aha!
    [*Bounding back*]
A hand-grenade! . . . No, no, my friend, I'm not
going to lose my other arm.

CAZOTTI [*Producing and re-pocketing it*]
It is an apple . . . I have had to eat as I could.

SALARET
Ah, like me when I lost my editorship. . . . Comrade
Vanni, withdraw you men, but if I sound the gong——

VANNI
The President strikes twice when he wants us to *rush*.
And there is his pistol on the table.

SALARET
Ah!

[*Seizes it as the* GUARDS *turn and go.*]

CAZOTTI
Put it down—you are such a bad shot, you might
really hit me. A pity you had no pre-revolution experience, like your aviating chief. See! I retire to this
pillar—whence Marrobio once addressed the Queen
Now you can listen calmly.

SALARET
I shall not listen long.

CAZOTTI
There is no need. One word of yours sufficed to show
me how the land lay.

SALARET [*Puzzled*]
What?

CAZOTTI
Precisely. The little word "What." When I mentioned the finances. You were not anxious I should
take them over.

SALARET
Why should I be?

CAZOTTI [*Blandly*]
I know I'm not such a *chartered* accountant as you are.

SALARET [*Fiercely*]
What are you hinting at?

124

CAZOTTI
Only the expense of carrying on your yacht's ducal tradition.

SALARET
Ducal tradition?

CAZOTTI
Come, come! You had your underground news-service before the revolution—we have it after.

SALARET
We?
     [*Strikes gong twice*]
I told Riffoni you were dangerous.
     [VANNI *and the* GUARDS *dash in.*]

CAZOTTI [*Coolly*]
And I once told him you were not.

SALARET [*Waving* VANNI *back*]
I was only testing your vigilance. Thank you.
     [*The* GUARDS *retire*]
So you admit you are here for treachery to the Republic.

CAZOTTI
And what name do you give to seducing the Republic's lady prisoners?

SALARET
What do you say?

CAZOTTI
I can speak louder if you like.

125

SALARET
No, no, I hear quite well—at least come a little closer.

CAZOTTI [*Coming almost up to him, sardonically*]
You see, how you are losing your alarm.

SALARET
Your news-service is false.   There are no women on
the yacht.   Riffoni will never believe you.

CAZOTTI
You may have smuggled them into safety—you could
hardly do less after your marine revelries.   But when
I call for the prison-records of the counter-revolu-
tionaries and ask where are such and such highborn
ladies, awaiting trial or execution—well, if I rightly
understand the evolution of your Riffoni, that dynamic
visionary, that ascetic assassin——

SALARET
He wasn't always such a saint.   What good would it
have done to shoot all those beautiful women?

CAZOTTI
Oh, don't suppose I utterly condemn you.   You had
a hard plodding youth, and a big dull family that you
couldn't always feed, and suddenly you find yourself
riding on the rainbow and commanding the eclipse.
You couldn't stand it, my friend, any more than those
highborn ladies could stand hunger and cold and the
fear of death.   I couldn't stand these things myself.
That's why I'm coming into your Government.

SALARET

You seriously insist——?

CAZOTTI

Government has become a habit with me—call it a vice. Without power I feel like the opium-eater without his drug.

SALARET

No! No! You shall not come in to betray Riffoni. Rather will I tell him everything. After all there's only one woman now, and I'm ready, nay anxious, to marry her.

CAZOTTI

It takes three to make a marriage and Signora da Grasso is still alive. But who says I come in to betray Riffoni? I come in to escape eating apples and creeping about like a hunted cat. There used to be flags and red carpets when I arrived at a town, every street grew full of pointing fingers, the place, however important, became a mere background for my personality. Now a pointing finger would be an arrow at my heart. It is not pleasant.

SALARET

I could smuggle you out of the country on the yacht—with a countess or two, if you like.

CAZOTTI

I don't. This is my year of mourning for my wife.

SALARET

You are a strange man.

127

CAZOTTI
I want my drug!

SALARET
Join Roxo—the Rolmenians will give you plenty of power.

CAZOTTI
Ah, but I want this new and concentrated form of it—decrees, ukases, rules, regulations, registrations, restrictions, prescriptions, perquisitions, inquisitions, raids, confiscations, censorship, compulsory labour, dictation at the bayonet's point, without public meetings, without newspapers, without parliaments—ye gods, what a flavour! How does it taste, Comrade, how does it taste?

SALARET
You exaggerate our autocracy as you caricature its object. If we take power, it is for social construction. You would take it as a drug.

CAZOTTI [*Chuckling*]
But not as an aphrodisiac.

SALARET
Damn you for a devil!
    [*Re-enter* RIFFONI *through the curtains.*]

RIFFONI
A devil indeed! When he offered to betray the Queen he knew she was already in our hands.
128

SALARET
We have the Queen?

RIFFONI
And the Duke D'Azollo! And the printers of the
Sera! As I suspected, the gang clung together. And
Komak nearly got this rascal too, who was on a visit
to the house, only he cunningly passed himself off as
President of the House Committee.

SALARET
The Queen has been in Scaletta all along?

RIFFONI
In the very heart. In an upper apartment belonging
to Brio's mother. The printing-press was in the loft.
Ah, Salaret, this is a great moment—second only to
that when we first stood here—you and I—in a Palace
purified of Queen and Court. Embrace me again,
dear Master.
    [THEY *kiss each other*]
Ah, how they melt away, all the obstacles to your
noble purpose! It is the compensation of your long
joyless years. . . .
    [CAZOTTI *has turned pale, but with arms folded
    strives to meet* SALARET'S *averted eye.* HE *now lets
    a little snigger escape him.* RIFFONI *turns on him*]
As for this dog, he said he began on a doorstep, let
him end high on the gallows. The Tribunal must sit
at once. Where is Vanni?
    [*Picks up his gong-stick.*]

SALARET [*Clutching the gong-stick*]
But, Vittorio, you said it was dishonourable to hang
him.

RIFFONI [*Pulling his stick back*]
Only if we had accepted his information. . . . Ah,
Salaret the Soft, when it comes to the point you can't
bear even a spider stamped on. You will next be
pleading for the Queen.

SALARET
The Queen is an encumbrance: Cazotti, you urged,
may be an asset.

RIFFONI [*Dazed*]
But it was you who—why I just heard you call him
a devil!

CAZOTTI
Because I mocked at your amateur Socialism. If I
couldn't make a better State than that, well, I shouldn't
wait for *you* to hang me.

RIFFONI
We know it is rough and ready.

CAZOTTI
Rough because *you* were not ready. Believe me, I
studied the Professor's books and bought your paper
regularly, but never did I see any imaginative grasp
of the new order, or the new evils that would arise
in place of the old, as the dint in an india-rubber ball
varies its place as you try to squeeze it away. You
foresaw nothing, prepared nothing.

130

RIFFONI
We cross our bridges when we come to them.

CAZOTTI
And they break down under you.   And your boats
you had already burnt.

RIFFONI
When Michael Angelo was asked how it was possible
to paint frescoes on the ceiling of the Sistine Chapel,
he replied the work itself would teach the method.
We live from day to day.

CAZOTTI
And from hand to mouth apparently.   Communism
forsooth!   You had to offer money even for my arrest
—enriching some individual!

RIFFONI
It's not so easy to abolish money.

CAZOTTI
No—it remains the root of all evil.   Well, I congratu-
late the anti-Socialists.   Your State is splendid adver-
tisement for them.

RIFFONI [*Piqued*]
What would *you* do?

CAZOTTI
When the physician is called in, he will prescribe.

SALARET
Do call him in, Riffoni—his very mockerey convinced
me of his sincerity.

131

RIFFONI [*Dazed*]
You are convinced of his sincerity?

SALARET
Absolutely.

RIFFONI
Then convince me of yours — give him over the Finances.

SALARET
With enthusiasm.

RIFFONI [*Taken aback*]
Although you know he was with the Queen this very morning?

CAZOTTI [*Glibly*]
I went to inform her of my change of views — to counsel her to quit Valdania.

SALARET
That was only fair.

RIFFONI [*Slowly*]
Well, Comrade Cazotti, this is a strange turn in the situation. *Would* you undertake the Finances?
    [SALARET *looks at* CAZOTTI *wistfully.*]

CAZOTTI
The problems of the Interior tempt me more.

SALARET [*In grateful admiration*]
Just as you please. . . .
    [*Holds out his hand, which* CAZOTTI *grasps. Enter*
132

OMAR *bearing a luncheon tray with three covers and a bottle of champagne, supplementing the Water-bottle.*]

RIFFONI
How the morning flies!
[*To* CAZOTTI]
You will join our repast?

CAZOTTI
With the greatest hunger.

RIFFONI [*Smiling*]
Luckily you come in for Colonel Molp's rations.   He had to go off.

CAZOTTI
Colonel Molp?   He has seen the light too?   Bravo!

RIFFONI [*With sudden rage to* OMAR]
Why have you brought champagne?

OMAR
Signor Salaret's orders, Effendi.

SALARET
To celebrate my return.   Why let the royal wine spoil in the cellars?

RIFFONI
We agreed it was to be used in the hospitals.

SALARET
That only resulted, I found, in the hospital staff getting drunk.

133

CAZOTTI [*Laughingly*]
Didn't I say the problems of the Interior were
tempting?

RIFFONI
This is no laughing matter. I see we must prohibit
alcohol altogether.

CAZOTTI
But not on the day of the Queen's capture! I do
hope it's the special vintage presented to her by the
King of Rolmenia—just before he declared war.

SALARET
We ought to have sent *you* to the cellar.

CAZOTTI
I was expecting to be sent lower still. And the dungeon
is deplorably out of repair. Ugh!

SALARET
Trust Omar to choose a good wine—wasn't he with
Gripstein?
> [OMAR *has meantime opened the bottle and poured
> out two glasses, but* RIFFONI *stops him at the third,
> which he fills himself from the water-bottle and
> raises in a toast.*]

RIFFONI
To our Triumvirate!

CAZOTTI [*Clinking a champagne glass with* RIF-
    FONI'S]
And the Workers' Republic!

134

SALARET [*Clinking both glasses*]
To the Workers' Republic!
> [THEY *drink. A confused sound of cavalry and
> shouting from the Piazza.* RIFFONI *drops his glass,
> which breaks.*]

RIFFONI [*Rushing towards the casement*]
Ah, at last!

CAZOTTI [*Amazed*]
You haven't had the Queen brought *here?*

RIFFONI
Where else?

CAZOTTI
The Fort Prison, of course.

RIFFONI
Right away on the lake? No, no. After the long
strain of awaiting her capture, I must have her under
my own eye.

CAZOTTI
But where will you put her?

RIFFONI
There is a dungeon.

CAZOTTI
Madness! I beg your pardon, but prisoners are my
department. You don't want the anti-Socialists to
go on congratulating themselves. Who has her old
suite?

135

RIFFONI
Salaret.

CAZOTTI
Salaret?   What is he doing in a woman's apartment?
[*Hurries through the curtains.*]

SALARET
Oh, Vittorio!   Suppose he should connive at her
escape.

RIFFONI [*Impatiently*]
You veer round like a child's toy.
[HE *throws open the casement, revealing the lake
and the snow mountains*]
Listen!
[*From the Piazza mounts a loud booing, through
which penetrate cries of "Down with Margherita,"
"Death to Margherita."   A voluptuously vindic-
tive smile slowly illumines his ascetic features as
the curtain falls.*]

ACT THREE

[*The same, the next morning.* COLONEL MOLP *stands showing* OMAR *a photograph.*]

MOLP

Intelligent? She's wonderful! Why, her grand-mother writes——

[*Pauses to press the picture to his lips.* RIFFONI *dashes in between the pillars clad in his airman's costume.* MOLP *slips the photograph away.*]

RIFFONI [*Throwing his cap and coat to* OMAR, *who goes out with them*]

Don't be so shy—I know it's only little Nina . . . Ouf, I wish I hadn't left word I'd call on Comrade Margherita at ten. I had to fly back just when I espied the Rolmenian vanguard.

MOLP

What a pity! For Her Majesty—er—Comrade Margherita—begs to be excused. She cannot receive you this morning.

RIFFONI [*Angrily*]

Eh?

MOLP

She has a headache.

RIFFONI [*Furious*]

Those feminine headaches! She had one yesterday, and she'll have one to-morrow—and for as long as

137

we leave her head on her shoulders. Did she look headachy?

MOLP
I saw only Signora da Grasso.

RIFFONI
Ha! In providing her with a Dame of Honour we have supplied her with a medium for her mendacity. I told Cazotti it was a mistake to continue this fairy-tale ritual. She should have had the dungeon for her boudoir, with the rats for courtiers.

MOLP
What have her courtiers proved but rats?

RIFFONI
Not all. More died for her than she deserved. I at least have no obligation to put up with her majestic megrims. Tell her I must insist on paying my respects.

MOLP
Respects? . . . Yes, my President.
  [*Going towards the curtains.*]

RIFFONI
One moment, Molp. Now that the last of the Whites are accounted for, we shan't need the guards, even in the corridor.

MOLP [*Alarmed*]
Oh, but you mustn't withdraw Vanni entirely.

RIFFONI [*Smiling*]
I won't—nor my confidence in you.
  [*Lays hand amicably on his shoulder*]
I was only testing you.

MOLP [*Wounded*]
You had my word.

RIFFONI
But the Queen is terribly fascinating—remember
Fiuma—and you seemed so moved, so solicitous.

MOLP
She is so young, so pitiable.

RIFFONI
Oh, you soldiers! You wouldn't be so sypathetic if
she were ugly and coarsehanded, like a woman who has
worked for her food.

MOLP
If you doubt me, my President, let me resign.

RIFFONI
Ah, you want to get out of dragooning her—she must
be a witch . . . Hark you, Comrade, if you try any
tricks against the Republic——! . . . Forgive me, my
nerves are on edge. I didn't sleep last night . . .
When are you bringing little Nina to see me?

MOLP
I haven't brought her yet from her grandmother's.

139

RIFFONI
Ah, you are afraid the Rolmenians will really get to
Scaletta—don't deny it!

MOLP
Since our troops are retreating before them——!

RIFFONI
Faintheart . . . Ah, here is the new Commissary.
Look! There's cheerfulness for you.
[CAZOTTI *enters between the pillars, spruced up,*
clean-shaven and frock-coated, a portfolio under his
arm, and in his whole bearing the jocundity of a
salvaged skipper, his foot again on his quarter-
deck.]

MOLP
I will deliver your message to Comrade Margherita.
[*Exit to the interior.*]

RIFFONI [*Shaking hands*]
Good morning, Cazotti, you look yourself again.

CAZOTTI
And you look somebody else. What's the matter?

RIFFONI
Insomnia—and news from General Hussein that sent
me scouting at dawn. But read for yourself.
[*Tends war-report.*]

CAZOTTI [*Perusing it*]
Ah, Roxo and Igmor are a tough combination . . .
And Roxo was always clever with cavalry. But surely
this swift advance of theirs plays into your hands.

140

RIFFONI
How so?

CAZOTTI
Won't it soon bring them within range of your aerial
torpedoes? In fact Hussein ought to feign retreating
faster.

RIFFONI [*Startled*]
Feign retreating?

CAZOTTI
If you are sure the torpedoes are all-annihilating.

RIFFONI
Yes, but then our troops would be between them and
the enemy! And if some of the Kites fell short and
annihilated ourselves! . . . Besides, you can't put the
ranks in the secret. And imagine a demoralised army
falling back on Scaletta—they might sow panic and
revolution, paralyse even our Kite corps.
    [*Smiling*]
No, Cazotti, stick to the problems of the Interior.

CAZOTTI [*Opening portfolio*]
I've done so. I, too, haven't slept. Here are the
edicts I promised to draft for you.

RIFFONI
Already? You're a miracle. But leave them on my
table, will you—it is high time I ran over to the War
Office to wire Hussein my ideas.

141

CAZOTTI

I am astonished at his giving way so—it was I that originally promoted him, despite the anti-Moslem prejudice. But do sign these at once.

RIFFONI

I must study them—wait five minutes, please.
[*Hurries out through the curtains.* CAZOTTI, *rather annoyed, steps on the dais to deposit the edicts.* VANNI *appears at the pillars.*]

VANNI

Oh, Excellency, for the blessèd Mary's sake——!

CAZOTTI [*Turning*]

Such words here?

VANNI

It was a slip of the tongue, Excellen—Comrade. But Stefano—they're hanging him to-morrow! And you promised——!

CAZOTTI

When I said I'd get your brother-in-law off, I didn't know that besides making brooches he sold them with the Queen's head.

VANNI

It was only the old stock, Excellency. He didn't like to waste them. And he lost an eye in the Bosnavian war.

CAZOTTI

But if the Tribunal condemned him——!

142

VANNI
They didn't dare not to——
    [*Lowers his voice*]
The President is so jealous of the Queen's pictures.

CAZOTTI
And I don't dare, either.   What would the People
say?

VANNI
But they're saying it's a bloody shame.   Oh!
    [*Claps his hand to his mouth.*]

CAZOTTI
Then why don't they say it aloud?

VANNI
Oh, your Excellency, if we only whisper, we feel the
flies are listening.   Our shadows seem like spies follow-
ing us.   His wife's the only one who won't keep her
mouth padlocked—in fact Fenella's been trying to turn
my own men against the Government—if it wasn't for
pity of her hysterics, they'd have denounced my poor
sister.

CAZOTTI [*Lightly*]
Then there's no chance of her turning them?

VANNI
Not while we get more grub than the civilians.
    [*Enter through the pillars* SALARET *bearing a port-
    folio, but minus his wonted spectacles.*]

CAZOTTI [*Loudly*]
Not another word, Corporal, it is impossible to raise your rations.

SALARET
Is he grumbling again?

CAZOTTI
Old soldiers always grumble.
[VANNI *sneaks backs to his corridor*]
But what's happened to you?

SALARET
Happened? Oh, you mean my spectacles! They broke, and the only decent opticians are dead or fled. Fortunately I can see to read or write, though I can't see far.

CAZOTTI
No—or you would have foreseen the flight of skilled labour.

SALARET [*Angrily*]
Have done! I have had enough of your criticisms. And, short-sighted as I am, I can see you are here to help the Queen.

CAZOTTI [*Enjoying himself*]
Lynx!

SALARET
Why else did you rush to receive her yesterday?

CAZOTTI
But I haven't even seen her yet—nor D'Azollo either.

I merely made arrangements for them. As a matter of fact, it will be rather awkward to meet my fellow-refugees.

SALARET
But Signora da Grasso—last night when you suggested my smuggling her over from the yacht for the Queen's service, I was grateful to you for fascilitating our romance. But on reflection I saw you were making things easier for the Queen, not for me.

CAZOTTI
I am making them easier for myself. I couldn't risk having one of my prisoners gallivanting on a yacht. Riffoni might have strung me up at your side—Comrade.

SALARET
Riffoni has no time to visit yachts.

CAZOTTI
But somebody might have put him on the scent—and the lady has a strong one. . . .
    [Sniffing]
Phew! You must have slept in the Palace!

SALARET [Tugging at his beard]
How you try to nose out everything!

CAZOTTI
Better I than Riffoni. The lady understands, I hope, she is supposed to have come straight from prison.

145

SALARET
Armida is prudent.

CAZOTTI
Armida? Ha! ha! ha! And does she call you Rinaldo?

SALARET [*Angrily*]
Youth is not the only quality that attracts a woman's sense of romance.

CAZOTTI
No—especially when she that loses her heart shall save her head. So you actually think she loves you for your beautiful eyes!

SALARET
I know it.

CAZOTTI
Aha! It is for her you broke your spectacles!

SALARET
You chaff like a college-student.

CAZOTTI
Why not shave off *your* beard and be as young as I?

SALARET
I am younger—a great passion rejuvenates.

CAZOTTI
Yes, to second childhood. Fancy putting yourself in the power of your own subordinate, the Commissary of Police!

SALARET
But Komak is in *my* power too.

CAZOTTI
You knew he was bribed not to find the Queen?

SALARET [*Startled*]
You know?

CAZOTTI [*Laughingly*]
Considering it was I who paid him his monthly
subsidy from Gripstein!

SALARET
Of course—I am stupid. . . .
   [*With sudden alarm*]
But you won't give him away now? If he were
arrested, he might round on *me*.

CAZOTTI
Highly probable. No, I won't give him away—it is
much more useful to have him in my pocket. But you
will scarcely expect me to believe in your devotion to
the Republic!

SALARET
I never attached importance to the Queen's capture—
indeed it only saddles us with a problem. But Riffoni
was always so obsessed about her.

CAZOTTI
Aha! *Cherchez la femme* in a double sense, eh?

SALARET
More college humour—you rightly said he's an ascetic.

147

CAZOTTI

So were you—till you were tempted. I expect she injected the fire when he saw her at Gripstein's.

SALARET

Don't be absurd, I tell you. He hates women, the Queen most of all.

CAZOTTI [*Going towards curtains with his portfolio*]

Well, anyhow, keep Armida out of his way.

SALARET [*Scandalised*]

Signora da Grasso?

CAZOTTI

He's been noticeably restless since her aroma permeated these corridors.

SALARET

You are trying to make me jealous—to divide us and rule.

CAZOTTI

Owl! I meant he might get wind of your relations.

SALARET

Armida is prudent, I tell you. . . .

[*With renewed alarm*]

Oh, but D'Azollo—you didn't tell him about——?

[*Pauses syly.*]

CAZOTTI

About his yacht? How shocked the old penitent would be to learn it is still the seat of Satan! But calm yoursel—knowledge is power, and I had so little power

148

just then I kept all I had to myself. . . . But soft!
I smell brimstone . . . !
 [HE *moves aside to let* SIGNORA DA GRASSO *enter.*
 SHE *sweeps by him in all her exotic beauty, natural
 and artificial*]
Good morning, Signora da Grasso!

ESTER DA GRASSO [*Turning with feigned surprise*]
You *here*, Count Cazotti?

CAZOTTI
Didn't Salaret tell you?

ESTER DA GRASSO
Salaret?

CAZOTTI [*Impishly*]
My colleague—Let me introduce you.

ESTER DA GRASSO [*Taken in by his blandness and
 bowing slightly*]
How do you do, Signor Salaret?

SALARET [*Furious, but restraining himself*]
I hope you slept well.

ESTER DA GRASSO
Beautifully, thank you. Such a change from the
prison. . . . So, Count Cazotti, you've turned Red.

CAZOTTI
I thought *you* would, when he asked how you slept.
149

ESTER DA GRASSO [*Blushing and disconcerted*]
He knows?

SALARET
I've already damned him for a devil.

CAZOTTI
Ha! ha! ha! . . . Armida is prudent.
[HE *moves laughingly towards the curtains, but, as
with a sudden thought, turns and goes out the other
way.*]

SALARET [*Approaching* ESTER]
Don't look so upset, *carrissima*.   I've sold him my
soul for his silence.
[*Tries to take her hand.*]

ESTER DA GRASSO [*Snatching it away*]
Let me be!   Why didn't you warn me? . . . Where
is Riffoni the Red?

SALARET
Sh!   What do you want of him?

ESTER DA GRASSO
The Queen sent me to say she prefers to come to *him*.

SALARET
Really?   Why should she humiliate herself?

ESTER DA GRASSO
It's pride, not humility.   She won't have her apartments profaned by the brute's presence.

150

SALARET
Hush, I tell you.

ESTER DA GRASSO
Oh, you are always a jelly before him. Hardly
Rinaldo's way, was it?

SALARET
You don't understand. I care for Vittorio and I care
for our Republic.

ESTER DA GRASSO
Yes, for everything except me.

SALARET
You know that's not true.

ESTER DA GRASSO
It *is* true—you let that cad Cazotti insult me.

SALARET
He insulted me too: we can only comfort each other.
    [*Throws down his portfolio*]
Give me a kiss.

ESTER DA GRASSO [*Recoiling*]
Aren't you sated yet?

SALARET
My love is infinite.

ESTER DA GRASSO
Yes, without beginning.

151

SALARET

After I've put away my glasses to please you!
    [*Seizes her hands*]
Just one!

ESTER DA GRASSO [*Wriggling her face from his
    lips*]
Not here!

SALARET [*Facetiously*]
Well, *there!*
    [*Dabs a kiss on her neck, while her face shows
    disgust*]
Why, you seem all strange. . . . Ah, you've changed
your scent.

ESTER DA GRASSO

I've tried to wash it all away—the Queen didn't like it.

SALARET

That profaned her chamber, too, confound her?

ESTER DA GRASSO

It aggravated her headache, poor thing. Are you
going to murder her?

SALARET

Ask the President. It's job enough to keep *you* alive.
Even before the Revolution you helped your husband
to shoot down his peasants, and the fact that he has
escaped only makes the mob bitterer against you. Sh!
I hear Vittorio's footsteps.
    [THEY *move apart*. RIFFONI *re-enters by the cur-
    tains, sniffing involuntarily.*]

152

RIFFONI
Good morning, Salaret. . . . Who is this lady?

SALARET
The Dame of Honour Cazotti selected from the
prisoners. She says the Queen wants to come to *you*.

RIFFONI
Aha! Margherita begins to understand our relative
positions.
[*Eagerly*]
When will she come?

ESTER DA GRASSO
At once, Signor.

RIFFONI [*Recoiling*]
No, no, I can't see her now.
[*Ascends the dais and takes up* CAZOTTI'S *drafts*]
I have my work. I will send for her when I want her.
Tell her so.

ESTER DA GRASSO
I will—but not in that tone.
[*Sweeps out haughtily, her lips moving vitupera-
tively.* RIFFONI, *plunging resolutely into* CAZOTTI'S
drafts, pays no attention to her.]

SALARET [*Uneasily covering her defiance*]
A beautiful creature, is she not?

RIFFONI [*Not looking up*]
So far as I remember.

153

SALARET
Remember? Why, you've just seen her.

RIFFONI
Oh, you mean that enchantress!

SALARET [*Crestfallen*]
You don't admire her?

RIFFONI
One can see you've broken your glasses. A woman
whose sex reeks and shrieks at you, the quintessence
of that sinister force that perverts thought and saps
purpose; one of the worst incarnations of the old
order. Hardly a fit companion for a presumably
virgin Queen. . . . Where's Cazotti? I asked him
to wait.
    [*Rings violently.*]

SALARET
He went that way . . .
    [*Moves towards pillars*]
Ah, he is talking to Vanni.
    [*Enter* OMAR.]

RIFFONI
Tell Comrade Cazotti I am back. He is in the
corridor.
    [OMAR *salaams and exit*]
If you had done your duty, Salaret, she would have
been executed long ago.

SALARET [*Startled*]
I couldn't help the Queen's not being caught before.
154

RIFFONI
Who is speaking of the Queen? I mean that scented
Signora—why have you kept her untried all these
months?

SALARET [*Tugging at his beard*]
Hers was merely a case of preventive arrest—if I
remember aright. . . . Or was she a hunger striker
too ill to be tried?

RIFFONI
A hunger-striker? Ha! ha! ha! Happily the Home
Department is in sterner hands now.
    [*Enter* CAZOTTI *with* OMAR, *who goes back.* RIFFONI
    waves a draft]
Ah, Cazotti, we were just talking of hunger-strikes.
And your hunger lock-out will be such a logical counter.

CAZOTTI
You've hit off my programme precisely. Logic—that
is what I want our State to exemplify.

SALARET [*Taking the draft uneasily*]
What is this hunger lockout? . . . Our peasants
work splendidly.

RIFFONI
And grow their own food. You can't cut off *their*
rations. But in the towns, the slackers, strikers, and
those who won't work on Saints'-days——

SALARET
Madness! There's too much logic already, Vittorio—
you're only too blind to life.

155

RIFFONI
I like that! When I follow your books!

SALARET
My books are pure mathematics. But life, like practical engineering, is applied mathematics—it has to take count of the obstacles and materials.

CAZOTTI
Surely our workers must be taught that now our workshops are nationalised, they have no more right to strike than a soldier to mutiny. A Workers' Republic that won't work is beyond a joke.

SALARET
But you have to deal with myriads. Even Roxo couldn't shoot down a battalion.

CAZOTTI
No, but he would have shot down every tenth man.

RIFFONI
That is an idea. Even though the enemy is on our soil, the turnout of the Kite-factories is in inverse proportion to the demand for rations and wages. It is high time the masses should realise that there is no inexhaustible source of wealth to be perpetually parcelled out, that the storehouse once emptied can be refilled only by their own labours——

CAZOTTI [*Blandly*]
Perhaps you didn't realise it yourself, while the cupboard was full. But now the logic of legislation must meet the logic of facts.

SALARET
Too much logic is simply dynamite.

RIFFONI
And doesn't the practical engineer use dynamite?

SALARET
You will blow up the State.   But perhaps that's what Cazotti wants.
    [*Throws down the draft angrily.*]

RIFFONI [*Pained and picking up the draft*]
Salaret, that is not fair criticism. . . . There's only one thing I must strike out of your draft, Cazotti, and that is the quotation from St. Paul—I'm afraid I can't cite that in my edict.

CAZOTTI [*Reading from the draft*]
"If any man will not work, neither shall he eat"? But surely that will bowl over the Cardinal.

RIFFONI
It will prop up St. Paul.

SALARET
The President is right.   Socialism will be suspected of Christianity.

RIFFONI
Then with your permission, Comrade Cazotti, out it goes.

CAZOTTI
Why, my permission?   The edict is your—I merely offer suggestions.

157

RIFFONI [*Striking out the quotation*]
Good! . . . Then here is my signature.
  [*Writes.* CAZOTTI *snatches at the draft*]
Wait, it'll smudge.
  [*Blots it,* CAZOTTI *is snatching at it again*]
Stop a moment! Does it say women-slackers shall be
locked-out too?

CAZOTTI [*Chuckling as he takes it*]
Trust me to give them full sex-equality.

RIFFONI
A pity you make us cocker Margherita so—I'd like to
see those white arms deep in the wash-trough.

SALARET
Don't be so truculent, Vittorio.

CAZOTTI [*Impatient to get his dynamite exploded*]
Would you mind signing the alcohol prohibition?
  [RIFFONI *becomes absorbed in the other draft.*]

SALARET
Has she really got such white arms, Cazotti?

CAZOTTI
The Queen? Oh, yes—she's beautiful enough if she
wouldn't look so gloomy.

SALARET
I've only seen her from afar like a shrined idol. Then
she isn't beautiful only by the royal standard?

CAZOTTI
The royal standard. Ha! ha! ha! Yes, it's pretty

low. The pig-eyes of Prince Igmor are "blazing orbs of war" in the Rolmenian literature.

RIFFONI [*Without looking up from the draft*]
And that's the man she was ready to sell her beauty to!

CAZOTTI
Fortunately I was able to stop the transaction. . . . Need you study it so minutely?
    [RIFFONI, *apparently re-absorbed, does not reply.*]

SALARET
They say her mother's marriage was a still more scandalous transaction.

CAZOTTI
What would you? Royal marriages are made in the War Office. But do you remember the sensation when King Tito brought home his northern bride?

SALARET
I was studying in Germany—I remember only the sensation at her murder.

CAZOTTI
Ah, that is another reason why we must go gingerly with the daughter. Margherita's trial must be solemnly staged at the High Court, with all deliberateness and dignity.

RIFFONI [*Flinging away his pen*]
Fiddlesticks!

CAZOTTI
I didn't know you were listening. But it is the only
159

possible course. Precipitation would seem assassination. Your crude new tribunals with their ranting amateur lawyers and their turbulent courts, from which the bourgeois are excluded—what you call the justice of the People——

RIFFONI [*Springing up*]
Then while your obsolete mummeries are preparing, the vixen who drew the sword of Alpastroom is to live in her Palace, the centre of a thousand secret sympathies!

CAZOTTI
Why did you bring her to the Palace? But as for sympathies, surely you heard the mob howling yesterday for her blood.

RIFFONI
Under the eye of Komak—I remembered afterwards——

CAZOTTI
Then if they really don't want her to die, why put her to death?

RIFFONI
All the more reason. Every day she breathes would be a breathing-space for the counter-revolution.

CAZOTTI
But also for the Republic. Once she is executed, you won't find even commercial dealings easy, especially with the king-ridden countries.

160

RIFFONI
Humph! What say you, Salaret?

SALARET
I understand Cazotti's point of view.

CAZOTTI [*Turning on him*]
What do you mean by insinuating——?

SALARET
Insinuating?

CAZOTTI
That I am trying to delay her execution!

SALARET
I never said so.

CAZOTTI
And that I am in secret communication with Roxo!

SALARET [*Sullenly*]
It is you who say it.

RIFFONI
Comrades, friends, what is the matter with you?

CAZOTTI
Salaret reeks with suspicions like Signora da Grasso with patchouli. I'd rather throw up my job—I can work only in an atmosphere of confidence.

RIFFONI [*Dominated and deprecatory*]
But all he said was he understood your point of view. And so do I—on reflection. A ceremonious State trial certainly—worthy of the dignity of the Workers'

Republic. Only let it be staged without delay. Will you see to the arrangements?

CAZOTTI

I suppose it falls within my department. . . . The alcohol prohibition still waits your signature.

[RIFFONI *sits and signs the second draft without further study and* CAZOTTI *blots and seizes it*]

Thanks! I'll have them both printed and placarded at once. Apropos, among a batch of misdemeanants sentenced yesterday afternoon and to be hanged tomorrow, I find that one lost an eye in the Bosnavian war. I propose to pardon him on that ground.

RIFFONI

By all means—and it will remind the People of the horrors of the old *régime*.

[*Takes a paper*]

I will sign the pardon at once.

CAZOTTI

Thank you. I don't need your signature.

SALARET [*Sharply*]

Why not?

CAZOTTI

Coming from the President, the pardon would savour of the bad old royal prerogative. Coming from me, it will seem to come from his comrades, the People!

RIFFONI

Cazotti is right.

162

CAZOTTI
Similarly should you be thinking of pardoning the
Duke——

RIFFONI [*Springing up*]
D'Azollo? *Corpo di Bacco,* I had forgotten all about
him!

CAZOTTI
Then I'm glad I reminded you, for his future too will
need settling.

RIFFONI [*Perturbed*]
Need one trouble about such a meagre future?

CAZOTTI
Once the Queen is disposed of, reaction may take *him*
for its focus.   Remember he has been Regent.

RIFFONI [*Drops on the throne again*]
You are always right.   Ah, what a comfort to have
your solid intellect to rest on—especially on a day when
I seem unable to fix my thoughts.
    [*Strikes the bell. Enter* OMAR]
Find Colonel Molp and ask him to bring the Duke
D'Azollo.
    [*Exit* OMAR, *salaaming.* CAZOTTI *is following him*]
No, don't go, Cazotti.   I want you both to sit beside
me.

CAZOTTI
You are not going to try him now?
163

RIFFONI

Of course not. I suppose he, too, would be a High Court case.

[SALARET *seats himself on* RIFFONI'S *right*]

You take this chair, Cazotti, I want to impress him.

CAZOTTI

I have better things to do than impress an old dotard.

RIFFONI

Not such a dotard—it was his wit barbed the *Sera*. I recognized the D'Azollo sting.

CAZOTTI [*Moving away*]

But I *must* get these posted up.

RIFFONI

Very well—let me see a proof, though, first, especially of the drink decree. . . . But I warn you I have a weakness for the Duke.

CAZOTTI [*Going towards the pillared exit*]

That doesn't alarm me. I know that the greater your affection for a person, the more sternly would you guard the interests of the Republic. Am I not right, Salaret?

SALARET

Oh, damn the Duke!

CAZOTTI [*Laughingly*]

Precisely what I ask.

SALARET

The truth is, Vittorio, Cazotti is ashamed to meet him.

164

CAZOTTI
Ashamed? I never said that.
   [*Turns indignantly and remounts the dais.*]

RIFFONI
I don't understand you to-day, Salaret.
   [*Strikes the gong once.* VANNI *and his men ap-
   pear*]
Stay here and salute Colonel Molp when he enters.

VANNI
Yes, my President.

CAZOTTI [*Taking his seat*]
Won't the Duke imagine the salute is for *him?*

RIFFONI
And if he does, poor old ruin? And don't you think
if we get his promise to accept the Republic——?

CAZOTTI
A promise? Fetters made of breath.

RIFFONI
Of the breath of a gentleman, Cazotti.

CAZOTTI
But his memory is so bad!

RIFFONI
Sh! His hearing is good.
   [*The curtains rustle, and* RIFFONI *on his throne
   between his two ministers takes a majestic pose,
   while the* GUARDS *stand rigidly.* SALARET *caresses
   his beard.* CAZOTTI's *aplomb seems for once to fail*

165

him and he rolls and unrolls his drafts. The DUKE *totters in, followed by* MOLP. *Though perceptibly aged,* D'AZOLLO *is the speckless old dandy of yore. The* GUARDS *present arms. The* DUKE *and* MOLP *acknowledge the salute.* RIFFONI *surveys his prisoner complacently for a silent moment*]
Well, Your Highness, I told you I should return.

DUKE D'AZOLLO [*Drily*]
Yes, I heard you were back.

RIFFONI
Ha! ha! ha! You haven't lost your wit—or your elegance. How do you manage it?

DUKE D'AZOLLO
These are the secrets of the bad old capitalist order—like courtesy to the aged and weary.

RIFFONI
I beg your pardon—give him a chair!
  [MOLP *hands the* DUKE *a chair.*]

DUKE D'AZOLLO [*Sitting down*]
Thank you! . . . And what do you propose to do with me?

RIFFONI
Humph! Not so easy as disposing of your yacht—my colleague, Professor Salaret, has put that to better uses than you ever did.

DUKE D'AZOLLO
I sincerely hope so. How do you do, Professor?

People known to the public are known to one another, as Euclid should have said. I have enjoyed your books—much more than Karl Marx's at any rate—and I am sorry our meeting in the flesh should be under such unhappy circumstances.

SALARET
They could not well be happier for *me*, Your Highness.

DUKE D'AZOLLO
I sit rebuked. But it is a consolation to see Cazotti in your ranks.

CAZOTTI
Eh?

DUKE D'AZOLLO
He will avenge us all!

SALARET
Ha! ha! ha! The Duke is in form.

CAZOTTI
The Duke is ungrateful. It is to my presence in the Government—if you will permit me to tell him so—that he and the Queen stand indebted for their considerate treatment. Let me tell him too that it is to him I owe my conversion to your form of Socialism.

DUKE D'AZOLLO
To me?

CAZOTTI
The wisdom you scattered at Baron Gripstein's—those little forgotten seeds have a way of germinating.

167

RIFFONI [*Eagerly*]
Ah, I remember! And since Your Highness favoured
Socialism platonically——?

DUKE D'AZOLLO
Quite the contrary. I distinctly remember leading
the debate for the negative.

RIFFONI
Where?

DUKE D'AZOLLO
At my University.

RIFFONI
I am speaking of a year ago, not a century.

DUKE D'AZOLLO
Santa Maria, my memory!

RIFFONI
You were ready to go up Mont Rouge—by telescope
at least.

DUKE D'AZOLLO
Ah, something begins to glimmer, God forgive me.

RIFFONI
And now that the mountain is scaled by foot—and the
Red Flag planted at the peak——

DUKE D'AZOLLO
But your State is an abomination. Without free speech
or free art or free movement! A dead-house!
168

RIFFONI [*Taking up a number of the* Sera]
Last month you called it only a forcing house.

DUKE D'AZOLLO
Did I? I am so glad. Yes, it is Socialism while you
won't wait. Not a Paradise of blossoming brotherhood, not a natural growth under God's heaven, but a
Socialism ripened prematurely under the heat of compulsion and watered with blood: a Socialism under
a sky of glass, unstable, sterile, without spontaneous
sap, that can be perpetuated only by ever-renewed
compulsion. And forced—good God!—from what
seed? Constricting figs in greenhouse pots will
precipitate them artificially, but there is high authority
for doubting if they can be gathered from thistles.
And human nature is unfortunately thistly. I speak
feelingly, for I was a forced child, artificially pietized
by a monastery of pedagogues. The result was the
sailing brothel that Professor Salaret has purged.

CAZOTTI
Ha! ha! ha! The Duke is in form.

SALARET
The Duke is in error. Our State is neither a dead-
house nor a forcing house but a school-house.

DUKE D'AZOLLO
I certainly see the rod.

RIFFONI
You used it to keep down the masses: we to educate
them. Did not Garibaldi, the champion of freedom,
169

say they could reach liberty only through dictatorship? Slave Socialism will beget free Socialism.

CAZOTTI
And don't forget, Duke, that to safeguard the young Republic, we have to live under martial law.

RIFFONI
Especially with Rolmenia never relaxing her attack.

SALARET
The censorship you jib at is merely the means to an end, and the end does not resemble the means any more than a fruit resembles its seed.

RIFFONI
But we won't be nipped in the bud by your aristocratic artists and thinkers!

DUKE D'AZOLLO [*Blandly*]
Are there any others?

RIFFONI [*Passionately*]
Their art is worthless. Art and Thought must be of the People.

DUKE D'AZOLLO
Good God! My peasants turned my library into cigarette-papers and my grand piano into a manure-sleigh. Aren't you satisfied with handing politics over to the People—the lowest thought of the greatest number!

CAZOTTI [*Seeing the others a bit disconcerted*]
The voice of the People is the voice of God.

170

DUKE D'AZOLLO
Then the voice of God needs training.

RIFFONI [*Unsmiling*]
Precisely. I knew you were with us at heart. Come,
Duke, I am sure we can find a formula to spare your
life.

DUKE D'AZOLLO
My life! What do these dregs matter? Ah, Vittorio,
if you must take vengeance on the old order, let *me*
be its representative, not the Queen.

RIFFONI
You offer your dregs for her brimming sparkle?

DUKE D'AZOLLO
Alas, it is all I can offer.

RIFFONI
You have nothing to offer. Your life is separately
forfeit to the Republic. If you wish to redeem it, you
must recognise that the old order is dead.

DUKE D'AZOLLO
Dead? Scarred perhaps, but titanically strong and
crafty, like one of those great old whales that go
careering about the oceans, stuck full of harpoons.
Believe me, Capital has a long swim before it, and
will yet upset your boat with a flick of its mighty tail.

RIFFONI
I only ask *you* not to bore holes in the boat. Give me
171

your word and you go free, with undisturbed possession for life of your town house at least.

CAZOTTI
A too generous offer.   But I am ready to write you a free pardon.

DUKE D'AZOLLO
God forgive you! . . . . You say, Vittorio, I repudiated Capitalism?

RIFFONI
Yes, at Gripstein's.

DUKE D'AZOLLO
Who wouldn't repudiate it *there?* . . . But did I ever repudiate my Queen?
   [*Anxiously*]
Tell me that!

RIFFONI
I am afraid not.

DUKE D'AZOLLO
Thank God!   Then, Vittorio, it all depends on whether you will give up that seat to her.

CAZOTTI [*Dropping his drafts*]
Put her back on the throne?

RIFFONI
You can't have a Queen in a Socialist State.

DUKE D'AZOLLO
Why not?

172

RIFFONI
It's a patent absurdity—unheard of!

DUKE D'AZOLLO
How conventional you are! But if there is no place
in your State for the Queen, there is none for me. I
go with her to the end.

CAZOTTI
Amen!
  [*picks up his drafts and remains standing*]
And now I suppose I may get on with my work.

RIFFONI [*Ignoring him*]
Then you would abandon the Duchess to a lonely old
age in an enemy country?

DUKE D'AZOLLO [*Eagerly*]
She has arrived in Bosnavina? You are sure?

RIFFONI
According to our Socialist spies, Gripstein's major-
domo smuggled her across the frontier.

DUKE D'AZOLLO
Well done, Brio! Ah, he was our good angel. He
even did the housework.

RIFFONI [*Smiling*]
In his white gloves? An excellent training for the
Workers' Republic. And Margherita, I suppose,
basked and purred by the fire.

173

DUKE D'AZOLLO [*Springing up*]
Speak more respectfully! Murder the Queen, but do not insult her.

RIFFONI
Speak more respectfully yourself. A State does not murder.

DUKE D'AZOLLO
Spare me verbal quibbles. Words were given us to drape our actions. Her Majesty did all we would permit her to do.

RIFFONI
Did she make her own bed?

DUKE D'AZOLLO
Yes, and my ailing wife's too.

RIFFONI
First Lady of the Bedchamber. Ha! ha! ha!

DUKE D'AZOLLO
Brio could have got her across the frontier at the same time as my wife, only she would not desert her country so long as there was any hope of helping it.

RIFFONI [*Meaningly*]
Ha! And I suppose *you* preferred to remain with *her!*

DUKE D'AZOLLO [*Re-seating himself placidly*]
Cazotti was so sure the Republic would collapse.

174

CAZOTTI
I? It was Gripstein who kept insisting it was bankrupt.

RIFFONI
Bah! Bankruptcy is only another way of spelling national debt.

DUKE D'AZOLLO [*Smiling*]
And in the end *we* were bankrupt—through Gripstein's arrest. That's why we were caught. . . . Oh, my memory! What have you done with the poor Baron?

RIFFONI
Don't worry—he won't stay poor long. How do you mean you were caught because you were bankrupt?

DUKE D'AZOLLO
Obviously we couldnt 'go on outbribing the reward on our heads.

RIFFONI [*Springing to his feet*]
Outbribing?

SALARET [*Tugging his beard*]
Our Commissary bribed? Impossible! Why, he——
    [*Stops short with a sudden perception he has said too much.*]

RIFFONI [*Thundering*]
Who is this dog?

CAZOTTI
That is the question. There are so many Police Com-

missaries. But of course you can't trust His Highness's memory.

DUKE D'AZOLLO
Not if you ask me his name—for I never knew it. But you ought to know, Cazotti, since it was you who paid his monthly account.

RIFFONI [*Turning fiercely on* CAZOTTI]
You paid him?

CAZOTTI [*Smiling sturdily*]
The finances always seem my job.

RIFFONI
You knew one of our Police Commissaries was a traitor and you failed to inform me?

CAZOTTI
Cazotti does not betray those who serve him.

RIFFONI
Then it seems he betrays those he serves.

CAZOTTI
Pardon me! My very first thought was to get rid of the rogue quietly.

SALARET [*Astounded*]
You have dismissed him?

CAZOTTI [*Dramatically handing* RIFFONI *a letter*]
Here is the letter I was just despatching. . . . No, no, give it me back. I forgot it has his name.
176

RIFFONI [*Refusing with a gesture and reading*]
Komak! . . . The Commissary in Chief!! Impossible!

SALARET
That's what I said. Komak is a pioneer of the faith—
my son's bosom friend.

RIFFONI
A serpent in the State's bosom!

DUKE D'AZOLLO
He! he! he! A very talking serpent. An agreeable
young rattle—a droll mixture of impulses. The day
he arrested us, he explained apologetically that he could
not afford to lose the reward—I understood he was in
collusion with a mock informant. He even kissed me,
maundering I reminded him of his aged father, and
he asked me for my blessing and forgiveness.

RIFFONI
Drunk into the bargain!

DUKE D'AZOLLO [*Shaking his head*]
Sober as a Moslem. I expect he had Bosnavinian
blood. They have this odd emotionalism. He even
wished to embrace the Queen.

RIFFONI
That's not so odd.

DUKE D'AZOLLO
Ah, but the tears were streaming down his cheeks. He
177

was so sorry he couldn't afford to give up the reward for her sake.

SALARET
The poor fellow must have needed money desperately.

RIFFONI
For orgies? . . . Was it you who appointed him? The wretch who failed to feed the children was also your selection.   You seem unfortunate——

SALARET
But for Komak's generosity Guido could never have invented the Kites.

RIFFONI
His generosity will not save him.

SALARET
It saved Gripstein.

RIFFONI [*Re-seating himself to fill up an order for arrest*]
There is no parallel between the cases.   Gripstein was an avowed enemy.

SALARET
My boy will be heartbroken.

RIFFONI [*Writing*]
I can well imagine it.   To lose at once his friend and his faith in him. What can be more tragic? Colonel Molp, escort the Duke to his room and see that this arrest is made instantly. . . . I am sorry Your High-
178

ness should have formed a mean opinion of the Republic's integrity—you will now witness its justice.

DUKE D'AZOLLO [*Who has risen*]
The test of a State is not the justice meted out to the guilty but the justice meted out to the innocent. Touch a hair of the Queen's head, Signori, and history will write you down poltroons and assassins.

CAZOTTI
Ah, but it is we who will write the histories now.
  [*The* DUKE *bows silently and totters out through the curtains, which* MOLP *parts for him.* CAZOTTI *holds out his hand to* RIFFONI]
Congratulations, Comrade!

RIFFONI [*Fiercely waving it aside*]
On what? On the rottenness of the Republic?

CAZOTTI
On your firmness with the Duke.

RIFFONI
The Duke? Did I decide about him? I am distracted. . . . Whom can I trust if a Komak fails me?
  [SALARET *rises*]
Where are you going?

SALARET
I feel I ought to see Komak safely arrested.

RIFFONI
Why? It is not your Department now. Molp won't

179

let him escape. Do sit down—there is so much to
discuss.

SALARET
But I have urgent financial business—there's a crisis.

RIFFONI
When Cazotti's accession has already put the exchange
up?
  [ESTER DA GRASSO *parts the curtains.* RIFFONI
  turns testily on her]
What is it now?

ESTER DA GRASSO [*Coming forward*]
Her Majesty begs you to receive her at once.

RIFFONI
I told you she must await my pleasure.

ESTER DA GRASSO
Waiting is so unnerving. She wants to get the interview over.

RIFFONI
I—I won't see her to-day at all.

ESTER DA GRASSO
That's a blessing.
  [*Turns to go.*]

RIFFONI
Insolence! Tell her she must come at once.
  [ESTER DA GRASSO *shrugs her shoulders and con-
  tinues her walk.*]

ESTER DA GRASSO [*At exit*]
I hope you will remember that Her Majesty has a headache.

RIFFONI
Corporal Vanni, take those men away!

VANNI
Right turn, quick march!
    [*Exeunt.*]

CAZOTTI
Why did you send them away?

RIFFONI
I thought they might salute her—or you suggest it.

CAZOTTI
They would have been as useful to impress her as to impress the Duke.

RIFFONI
I don't want to impress her.

CAZOTTI
Really? Then I suppose I can go.

RIFFONI
Ah, you *are* ashamed to meet your old friends.

CAZOTTI [*Wincing*]
I have my work.
    [*Exit* CAZOTTI *by the pillars, carrying the ukases.*
    RIFFONI *sits brooding darkly.* SALARET, *who has
    resumed his seat sullenly, is tugging at his beard.*]

SALARET
Vittorio, you surely won't press for the death-penalty?

RIFFONI
Why should she escape the doom of a Marie Antoinette?

SALARET
She? We are at cross-purposes to-day. I was speaking of Komak.

RIFFONI
Komak! You bring that up again!

SALARET
Only for my boy's sake.

RIFFONI
Were it Guido himself, I should string him up!

SALARET
Oh! . . . This is your friendship . . . And I, were I in your place——

RIFFONI [*Starting up*]
What a good idea! *Take* my place.

SALARET
Your place?

RIFFONI
Sit here and do the talking to the lady—what with the Duke and Komak on top of a sleepless night my nerves are on edge.

182

SALARET
Why not spare yourself then? There is no point in
our seeing her before the trial.

RIFFONI
None whatever. I will countermand her.
    [*Rings. Enter* OMAR]
Tell Signora da Grasso that I cannot—that—that she
is not to accompany her mistress.
    [*Sits down again shamefacedly.* OMAR *salaams
    and exit*]
I had to say something—you see, on second thoughts,
I felt the Queen would think me an irresolute idiot.

SALARET
You said you didn't want to impress her.

RIFFONI
But I don't want to feed her vanity—make her feel
irreplaceable! That's why I asked *you* to receive her
—I'm quite unstrung.

SALARET
But without my spectacles I won't even see her face
properly.

RIFFONI
All the better. It won't trouble your dignity.

SALARET [*Grudgingly*]
If I receive her, you must go and try to get a little
sleep.

183

That *would* be wisest. . . . No, I have a curiosity to
see the creature.   Come, sit there and I'll sit here.
> [*Motions* SALARET *to the throne and takes a chair
> on the far side of the table*]

She'll think I'm a secretary.
> [HE *seizes a pen and heaps up papers, partly hid-
> ing his face.*]

SALARET [*Seating himself gingerly on the throne*]
What on earth am I to say to her?

RIFFONI
What on earth does it matter?   We shall enjoy her
humiliation.

SALARET
I shan't—I shall feel uncomfortable, I know.   Surely
you can do the talking yourself.

RIFFONI
And if I do, who knows where my hate may carry
me?   I shan't stop at the mealy-mouthed courtesies
Cazotti would approve.   At my first meeting with her,
remember, I had to be dumb—that suppressed speech
has been boiling in my veins ever since.
> [*There is a stir in the corridor*—SALARET *leaves
> the throne hurriedly and sits to the right.*]

SALARET
I can talk just as well from here.   She might think I
was you.

184

RIFFONI [*Rising*]
Nonsense—trust her to have seen our pictures.
 [*Moves to the chair on the near side*]
I'd better sit here—then I'll have my back to her
when she comes in!

OMAR [*Parting the curtains*]
Way for the Queen!

RIFFONI [*Angrily*]
Why, who the devil told Omar——? . . . Quick!
Don't leave her throne empty!
 [SALARET *scuttles back into it and tugs his beard.*
 RIFFONI *again snatches a pen and heaps papers.*
 The QUEEN *enters slowly, sad, but with unbroken*
 dignity. SALARET *rises instinctively,* SHE *bows*
 silently. RIFFONI *is ostentatiously writing, but*
 with an obviously shaky hand.]

SALARET
Be seated, Madam, I am sorry I cannot offer you
your usual seat.

QUEEN [*Taking the chair vacated by the* DUKE]
You are welcome to it, Signor Salaret.

SALARET
Your Majesty's recognition flatters me.
 [*Re-seats himself*]
As you see I am deputising for the President; he is so
—overworked.

QUEEN
Please convey to him my appreciation of his courtesy
185

in the matter of my apartments. I had not expected it.

SALARET [*Stroking his beard*]
The Workers' Republic is much maligned.
    [*There is an awkward pause.* SHE *looks round*]
You find the Palace changed?

QUEEN
It looks so military.

SALARET
Military, Madam? Why, it was a positive barrack!

QUEEN [*Looking at the plain casement*]
At least the Madonna stood guard too.

SALARET
The Republic can dispense with her protection. . . .
But you can still find her undamaged in the Palace chapel. Access is not denied you, I believe.

QUEEN
There are no priests.

SALARET
You would not have us enthrone superstition in our own headquarters?

QUEEN
Is the worship of the People a nobler superstition than the worship of God?

SALARET
The People at least is a reality. And we can make it worthy of worship.

RIFFONI [*Murmuring*]
Bravo!
    [SALARET *frowns in his direction.*]

QUEEN
Ah, the Duke always says nothing can shake the credu-
lity of atheists. . . . What do you mean to do with
him?

SALARET
With D'Azollo? He will be tried like you.

QUEEN
Poor old man! What has *he* done?

SALARET
What has he left undone?

QUEEN
Cannot *my* death atone for his sins too?

SALARET
I did not say you would be condemned to death.

QUEEN
Do no rob me of my last hope.

RIFFONI [*Dropping his pen*]
Eh?

SALARET [*Equally amazed*]
You desire death?
187

QUEEN
"He giveth His belovèd sleep." O to be done with
the duty of living!
   [*Covers her eyes.*]

SALARET
Why should you wish to die?

QUEEN
Why should I wish to survive my friends? Ah, so
many have been sent behind the black curtain—Fiuma,
Marrobio, Livia, Gripstein——
   [*Her voice breaks.*]

RIFFONI [*Prompting* SALARET]
But Gripstein——

SALARET [*Annoyed*]
Yes, yes, I know. . . . Gripstein and the Baroness
have been spared, Madam. As for Marrobio, murdered by a Bosnavinian patriot, he fell a victim to
your imperialistic insanity.

RIFFONI [*Thumping the table*]
Bravo! Bravissimo!
   [*The* QUEEN *at last turns and looks in his direc-
   tion.*]

SALARET
Restrain yourself, Comrade. You have spilt the ink.

RIFFONI [*Hoarsely*]
What is her answer? You see she has no answer.

188

SALARET
What is your answer, Madam?

QUEEN
It was Bosnavina declared war. I had no more power
under my Government than I have under yours.

RIFFONI [*Springing up and facing her*]
It is false——!

SALARET [*Interjecting*]
Vittorio!

RIFFONI [*Fiercely uninterruptible*]
You drew the sword of Alpastroom, and girding it on
Marrobio, bade him win back your Bosnavinian
Duchy. What is your answer?

QUEEN [*Rising*]
I thank you, Signor Salaret, for your courtesy.
      [*Bows and moves towards the curtains.*]

RIFFONI
Stop, Madam!
      [SHE *moves disdainfully on.* HE *strikes the gong
      twice.* VANNI *and his* GUARDS *rush in.*]
Arrest her!

QUEEN [*Turning to face their bayonets*]
Corporal Vanni!
      [THEY *shrink back.*]

RIFFONI
Arrest that woman, I tell you.
      [THEY *surround her.*]

189

QUEEN [*Veering round to confront* RIFFONI]
Who are you that dare insult your Queen?

RIFFONI
That Queen's Master.

QUEEN
Ha! I thought you posed always in general's uniform. . . . So *you* are Riffoni the Red?

RIFFONI
Yes. Last time I was Riffoni the Silent.

QUEEN
Last time? We have met before?

RIFFONI
At Baron Gripstein's.

QUEEN
So the Duke always insisted—but I thought it was his bad memory.

RIFFONI
It was your own, Madam. And yet I flattered myself I had made an impression. For you pronounced me intelligent—intelligent enough for higher work.

QUEEN [*With a flash of remembrance*]
Ah, you were Molp's man!

RIFFONI [*Grimly*]
No, I was not Molp's man, but Molp is my man. I hope I have justified your flattering augury. Yes, intelligent as I was, I was thrust out of your realm

190

that night, torn from my friends, my work, deported like a criminal.

QUEEN
It is what you have proved, Signor.

RIFFONI
Have a care how you insult the Republic!

QUEEN
An intelligent criminal is worse than a criminal fool. And murder, pillage——

RIFFONI
Be silent, woman! . . . Withdraw, Vanni!
    [VANNI *silently marches his men out, while* RIF-
    FONI *without a pause continues vehemently*]
You to condemn murder, under whose rule I was first forced to kill! Ah, the nausea that overcame me when I had to send a brother-airman shrivelling to the ground like a burnt moth!

QUEEN
And was it not enough our land was torn by wars of race and wars of religion and wars of revenge, must you add the war of classes?

RIFFONI
And why may not war be waged perpendicularly as well as horizontally? The war of classes is the only war worth waging, the war for a righteous order, the war to end war. It is the horizontal wars of grab and glory that are immoral. Ah, what really excites the world's horror in our perpendicular campaign is that

it is a blasphemy against the great god, Money; that it is the wealthy we combat, those who made of the masses a footstool for their feet and a cushion for their backs. But if we make them suffer in their turn, it is not for revenge but to shape the brotherhood of all.

QUEEN

Brotherhood cannot be shaped by steel like a dead log. It must grow slowly like a living tree, fed by the dews and rains, ripened by the sun——

SALARET

Ah, the forcing house again! She is a gramophone for the Duke's platitudes.

QUEEN

The Duke is wiser than you both. But it is not from the Duke I have learnt this wisdom—it is from Vittorio.

SALARET [*Astonished*]

Vittorio?

QUEEN [*Producing a dainty little volume*]

I carry his songs with me night and day.

RIFFONI [*Dazed*]

You read my father's poems?

 [HE *descends almost unconsciously towards her.*]

QUEEN [*Equally amazed*]

Vittorio was your father?

RIFFONI
He wrote under his Christian name.

QUEEN
He wrote Christianly indeed.

RIFFONI
And was done to death in this Palace of yours. On
that balcony!
  [*Points to the plain casement.*]

QUEEN
I am glad he did not live to see his son do others to
death.

RIFFONI
They die that his ideas may live.

QUEEN [*Surveying the book*]
What a caricature of his doctrine of love!

RIFFONI
I deny it. Is love less love because like the sun it
wears a face of flame? Has not destruction also its
angel? This old malarial world needed a storm to
purify it, to uproot its monstrous millennial growths.
Ah, wait till the lightnings have ceased to sear, and
the storm has blown by, and you behold the blue of
the new heaven and the green of the new earth.

QUEEN
And how long must I behold only the red of your new
hell? This storm of yours, that hides heaven and

earth, will my death hasten its passing? Then kill me speedily in God's name.

RIFFONI [*Moving nearer to her*]
Why should the Workers' Republic kill you? Perhaps it can find work for you.

QUEEN
What place can there be for me among your sans-culottes and furies? No, no, if you would have me live, let it be far from you.

RIFFONI
What! Swell the camp of our enemy exiles in Bos-navina!

QUEEN
I should leave the Cockpit altogether—let me go to America!

RIFFONI
Aha, so that's the game, that's why old Gripstein was so anxious about his fare. So that great sentimental country is to espouse the cause of beauty in distress, its myriads of rich Valdanians are to write cheques and manifestoes for our destruction. No, Comrade Margherita, if you sincerely share my father's vision, your place is here, helping us to give it substance.

SALARET [*Starting up*]
Vittorio! What are you saying?

RIFFONI
It is the only solution. It will please Cazotti and his
194

Western friends. It will bring peace. D'Azollo will be saved. The Royalist exiles will troop back.

SALARET
Yes, to their estates and investments!

RIFFONI [*Furiously*]
I speak to the Queen!
  [SALARET *subsides on the throne.*]

QUEEN
But I loathe your methods, I tell you—how can I work with you?

SALARET
Or under what Constitution?

RIFFONI
Constitutions were made for States, not States for Constitutions. Let her style herself Queen for aught I care.

SALARET
Queen of the Republic? Ha! ha! ha!

RIFFONI
Am I not practically its King? You are so conventional, so afraid of words—ah, you were always a writer. All that matters is that we keep Comrade Margherita among us to inspire us with her noble outlook, to be the incarnation of our dreams, the Lady of our Republic. Come, what say you, Comrade Margherita?

QUEEN
I have answered you.

RIFFONI
Yes, you dislike our methods. But methods are provisional. The end we dream is the same.

QUEEN
I did not say that. Economic equality is not the light of the world nor even its sure happiness.

RIFFONI
It is the way of reason and brotherhood. Rations and rational are one at root. Shall mankind for ever scuffle for its food like a litter of swine? Ah, your love of my father's poems is as sterile as the Duke's Socialism. Too many idealists wish that idealism were practicable. Dare to face your own beliefs and to live them.

QUEEN
What is it you want? What is it you are proposing?

RIFFONI
I am proposing an alliance.

QUEEN
Between Monarchy and Republicanism? Is that feasible?

SALARET
The lady has more sense than you, Vittorio.

RIFFONI
Why do you interfere? All Europe shows alliances

between Monarchies and Republics. And when an
alliance between these systems is incarnated in
persons——

QUEEN
In persons?

RIFFONI
In you and me.

QUEEN [*Slowly, as his meaning begins to dawn on
her*]
In me—and you?

RIFFONI
Ah, you shrink. But you were ready enough for an
alliance with Prince Igmor?

QUEEN
You know that? . . . Then you know to what a hor-
rible political necessity I would have sacrificed myself.
They told me it was Valdania's only salvation.

RIFFONI
And may not *our* alliance be its salvation?

SALARET
Your destruction!

RIFFONI
Be silent!

SALARET
Reds and Whites would be equally revolted.

197

RIFFONI
On the contrary—they will be reconciled through us.

QUEEN [*Shuddering*]
God did not deliver me from Prince Igmor to hand
me over to Riffoni the Red.

RIFFONI [*Savagely*]
But He did, you see.

QUEEN
Let me die then. Your idea is monstrous. Even the
Rolmenian proposition was not so cold-blooded. There
was love on the Prince's side at least.

RIFFONI
And how do you know there is none on the President's?

QUEEN
On yours? Why, you hate me! You have scarely
seen me.

RIFFONI
My first glimpse was enough for hate at first sight—
does love need a prolonged stare? Nay, was it hate
you kindled in my veins, was it not perhaps love—
love all the fiercer for my hate of all you stood for?
Your beauty seemed as sinister to me as the blue
lake that had sucked down my little brother. But
who knows if it was not really your face that drew
me back from exile? Perhaps my whole Revolution
was only a bridge to span the gulf between us. Even
then you lurked uncaptured, forcing my thoughts to
198

dwell on you, and if I wrested them free from your image, it was only to meet it again in bust or picture, coin or stamp. And yet when you were at last under my roof — under *your* roof — under *our* roof — my yearning to see and face you was shot through with dread. I felt you were more terrible to my Republic than Roxo and all his Rolmenians. But now that I find you no goddess of war, but a friend of my father's dream, not treacherous like our lake, not fatal and sinister, but sweet and simple, I say to you, Margherita——

QUEEN [*Recoiling*]
Do not say it. The blood of my murdered friends cries out against my listening.

RIFFONI [*Exasperated*]
You must listen! If I have shattered your world to bits, it was only to remould it more justly.

QUEEN
The gasping for breath of a child I saw shattered here in your assault, refutes your loud-lunged logic.

RIFFONI [*Subdued*]
My logic may have led me astray. Perhaps I took the wrong turning to my father's Paradise. Your voice leads me back from that red road to his quiet footpaths—I hear the village church bells—Comrade Margherita, put your hand in mine——
    [*Holds it out.*]

199

QUEEN
I cannot.

RIFFONI
Not even to lead me in *your* way? Come!
    [*Grasps at her hand*]

QUEEN [*Dropping her book*]
Touch that hand stained with my people's blood?

RIFFONI [*Stung to frenzy*]
It is not the people's blood on my hand, it is the
plebeian blood in my veins. But by all your gods I
am a better man than your pig-eyed princeling. Your
hand, I say!

QUEEN
Never!

RIFFONI
Now!
    [*Seizes it.*]

QUEEN
Release me, Signor!

RIFFONI
Not till you——
    [SALARET, *who has sat spell-bound on the throne
    starts up and strikes the gong twice.* RIFFONI
    drops the QUEEN'S *hand.* VANNI *and his men rush
    in.* OMAR *appears at the curtains.*]

200

SALARET
Escort Her Majesty to her apartment.
> [*The* GUARDS *salute.* OMAR *rushes to pick up the*
> QUEEN'S *book and parts the curtains reverentially.*
> *Ceremoniously bowing to* SALARET, SHE *passes out*
> *with stately tread, followed by* VANNI *and his*
> GUARDS. RIFFONI *stands in silent impotent fury.*]

RIFFONI [*Turning on* SALARET]
How dare you interfere?

SALARET
I had to save you from yourself—and my Republic
from your folly.

RIFFONI
You are an old pedant with red ink in your veins.
This woman and I are mates—mates in body and
soul.

SALARET
But the woman loathes you.

RIFFONI
As I thought I loathed her. She is the counterpart
created for me—blood and spirit cry it together.
> [*Flings out through the curtains.* SALARET *lets*
> *himself fall into the royal chair, dazed. By the*
> *pillars* CAZOTTI *re-enters, carrying large placards.*]

CAZOTTI
Ha! ha! ha! What did I say?

201

SALARET
You heard?

CAZOTTI
Enough to grasp the situation. So you begin to see
your idol's feet of clay.

SALARET
When the idol loses his head, one naturally notices the
feet. As I sat here at his request, for he felt the sight
of his darling would un-king him, I found myself
endowed literally with a new point of view. And
looking down on him, as he grovelled before her, I
asked myself why I, the senior, should live like a
schoolboy under the preceptor's rod.

CAZOTTI
Especially when Komak's effusiveness might set the
rod swishing——

SALARET
Clairvoyant!

CAZOTTI
And Cazotti was at hand to snap it.

SALARET
Mind-reader!

CAZOTTI
Ha! ha! ha!
    [*Extends hand, which* SALARET *grasps*]
So it's a bargain. . . .
    [*Smiling*]

202

You don't remain in the chair, of course. . . . No, no hurry.

SALARET [*Rising*]
So long as I keep the yacht. . . . But I won't have Vittorio killed! You must deport him.

CAZOTTI [*Laughing*]
What again? Molp will get tired. . . . But we can't deport him yet. We need his military genius to destroy Roxo and the Rolmenians.

SALARET [*Dazed*]
Then you are not in league with them? You don't want to restore Margherita?

CAZOTTI
When I've just asked you for her chair?

SALARET
You? You wish to be *King?*

CAZOTTI
Don't you know the dose of the drug must always be increased?

SALARET
Then why do you postpone the Queen's execution?

CAZOTTI
How do you know *Roxo* won't win? Where should I be then? As it is, by restoring her to her rooms and keeping her untried, I have proved my loyalty.

SALARET
But what about me?

CAZOTTI
Haven't you just won her gratitude?

SALARET
But if Roxo is annihilated?

CAZOTTI
That is what I hope and believe, for then, with the
Queen already in our hands, we have only to get rid
of Riffoni.

SALARET
Those edicts of yours will do that, I know. But won't
we both blow up *with* him?

CAZOTTI [*Chuckling*]
Not while he signs the edicts and I the pardons.
Cazotti the Compassionate, eh? You are already
safeguarded as Salaret the Soft. Be faithful to me
and I will save you, even if Komak prove leaky. Nay,
for your boy's sake, I will save Komak himself, as I
have already saved Stefano.

SALARET
Are you sure you know your Riffoni? Have a care!
He is capable of turning suddenly like a bull in the
arena. With one bound he may unhorse us both.

CAZOTTI
Bah! Picador Cupid will weaken him hopelessly.
Already you have seen him quivering under the darts.

My only fear is lest he collapse before he has unhorsed
Roxo and Igmor.
    [*Sirens begin to sound*]
What is that?

SALARET
It must be the signal for my boy's Kite Corps.
    [*Bugles sound from the Piazza. Excursions,
    alarums.*]

CAZOTTI [*Troubled*]
The Rolmenians must have broken our line!

SALARET
I'm afraid so.
    [RIFFONI *rushes in through the curtains in his air-
    man's cap and coat, transfigured equally in bearing,
    waving a telegram.*]

RIFFONI
At last my strategy has come off!

CAZOTTI
Your strategy?

RIFFONI
The tactics you all but guessed at—to lure the enemy
within range of our Kites! But by letting them outflank us, not drive us before them! Roxo has fallen
into the trap and is advancing swiftly on Scaletta ar
annihilation.

205

SALARET [*Perturbed*]
But if the Kites fail! Surely you take a terrible risk.

RIFFONI
It is by taking terrible risks that I stand here.

CAZOTTI
Bravo!
  [*Grasps his hand*]

RIFFONI
Roxo is finely fooled. When he used to conduct the
manœuvres against King Tito, he always had to work
desperately to get the King to outflank him. Yet he
failed to see the same game was being played on himself.
    [*The faint strains of a band striking up the
    National Hymn ascend from the Piazza.*]

CAZOTTI
We must make Hussein a Marshal.

RIFFONI
Naturally. Ah, the sacred joy of battle for our flag!
She asperses our swords but they are holier than her
Madonnas, our Kites are more heavenly than her
angels. And to think that a moment ago I was pos-
sessed of a demon!

CAZOTTI
How do you mean?
206

RIFFONI
Salaret has not told you?

CAZOTTI
Oh, that! The thought of caressing a Queen flattered your senses for a moment, I never took it seriously.

RIFFONI
Thank you—you knew me better than myself. In that moment of clouded vision our Republic was in the balance, my granite plans ran like wax, and but for Salaret——
   [*Grasps his hand emotionally*]
Forgive me, dear saint, but—in that mad moment—to touch a shrinking hand seemed more wonderful than to build up a State for mankind.
   [*The bugle is heard more loudly*]
Ah, I thank the god of chance who sent me this stern reminder. Ouf! it is good to cast out the demon that has preyed on one's vitals, to feel free again, free to shape with steel and flame, a man among men!
   [*Grasps* CAZOTTI'S *hand also for a moment, uniting the triumvirate*]
Imagine it, Cazotti, her pose as a peace-lover deceived even me—I was fooled worse than Hussein fooled Roxo. I forgot that my first sight of her was in a colonel's uniform — now the wily female wears my father's *Songs of Brotherhood* next to her heart.

CAZOTTI
Ha! ha! ha! Why, her military ambitions were the worry of my ministry.

SALARET
The devil fell sick, the devil a saint would be.

RIFFONI
She is wilier than the devil—was she not brought up
in a Jesuit Convent? Though she had dodged capture
all these months, she pretended that death was her
dearest desire; and to set my palm itching worse for
her, she feigned to shrink from its bloody touch. Ah,
let her have the death she whined for—she is too
dangerous to live. We three, Cazotti, must adjudge
her doom forthwith—we can't await your ceremonial
tomfoolery.

CAZOTTI [*Taken aback*]
But my friends in the West——

RIFFONI
To hell with them all and damn diplomacy! We have
stood so far by our own brute strength. Force is all
that the West respects—only by ruthlessness can we
save our Republic from the foes without and the still
more dangerous foes within. Apropos, Cazotti, I veto
your pardoning the one-eyed malefactor. He must die
at dawn and Komak with him. And that signora and
the other ladies your softness has spared so long must
join their mistress on the scaffold. It will be her
escort of honour, ha! ha! ha! *A rivederci!*
    [*Hastens towards the pillars.*]

CAZOTTI [*Waving his placards*]
But these proofs!

RIFFONI

Read them yourself!

[*The bugle sounds a peculiar flourish*]

Do you hear? Our air-scouts have sighted Igmor's cavalry. I must be in at the death!

[*Exit hurriedly.* SALARET *looks at* CAZOTTI, *as though to say "I told you so."* CAZOTTI *shrugs his shoulders.*]

CURTAIN.

ACT FOUR

[*The same on a waning afternoon some weeks later. The table on the dais is heaped chaotically with correspondence, opened and unopened.* OMAR *and* VANNI *are conversing in low tones.*]

OMAR
Courage, friend, this is not like Allah's hell, in which one must remain for ever.

VANNI
I wish I had my two hands to strangle him with as he had Stefano strangled.

OMAR
You have twice as many hands as you have soldiers. But Captain Lambri is *their* job, remember.

VANNI
But can I rely on their hands, the swine? You see——
[*Enter* SALARET *hurriedly through the pillars.* HE *is spectacled once more.*]

SALARET [*Suspiciously*]
Why are you not at your posts?
[*They are sneaking out in opposite ways*]
Stop, Omar! I want you to go to the Queen's apartments and send Signora da Grasso here.

OMAR
Yes, Effendi. But without a pass Captain Lambri won't let even her shadow cross the doorstep.

SALARET
These men of the Left Wing are very tiresome.

OMAR [*Murmuring*]
May they drink boiling water!
[SALARET *clears a space at the table, bends down
and writes.*]

SALARET
Here you are!
[OMAR *takes the pass, salaams and exit.* SALARET
*goes to the plain casement and throws it open, re-
vealing the lovely blue lake backed by snow-moun-
tains.* HE *peers out sideways*]
Ah, you can just see her funnels.
[*With a sudden thought* HE *slips off and hides his
spectacles. A band in the Piazza below strikes up
a march and troops are heard swinging forward
to it*]
Already?
[HE *closes the window. The curtains part rustling.*
HE *turns eagerly, but his face falls to see only* OMAR
re-entering.]

OMAR
The Signora refuses to come.

SALARET
Refuses? You should have fetched her by force!

OMAR
Bismillah! It is not *my* harem.

212

SALARET
Insolent! . . . I *must* see her before the President
returns.
[SIGNORA DA GRASSO *appears at the curtains*]
Ah, the Signora has changed her mind.

OMAR
I am your humble servant who kisses the hem of your
garment.
[*Salaams and exit.*]

SALARET [*Advancing*]
At last, *carissima!*

ESTER DA GRASSO [*Retreating*]
Keep your distance. You know you have grown ab-
horrent to me, that even your letters are returned,
unopened.

SALARET
Because you make me responsible for the Queen's con-
demnation. As if——!

ESTER DA GRASSO
A truce to words. I have come only to find out why
these soldiers are marching. Our guards, who tell
me everything, seem tongueless when Captain Lambri
is on the pounce. Does it mean Riffoni is returning?

SALARET
That's why I sent for you. They're off to the station
to welcome him.

213

ESTER DA GRASSO
Mother in heaven! Then he has crushed the rural
revolution?

SALARET
As completely as he asphyxiated Roxo and the Rolmenians. He has forced the villages to divide their
crops and cattle with the towns, and will thus regain
in the towns the prestige imperilled by his edicts and
executions.

ESTER DA GRASSO
He has the devil's own luck.

SALARET
But the angels' luck can be ours, Armida. Listen!
    [Lowers his voice]
The yacht is ready to sail. Ever since the news of
his return came this morning, I have been secretly
provisioning it with food and gold. . . . Get your hat
and cloak—enough of your things are still there.

ESTER DA GRASSO
Sail with you?

SALARET
Without a moment's delay. We will steam down the
river to the Mediterranean, and then hey for the
magic islands!

ESTER DA GRASSO
You would abandon your precious Republic and your
precious President?

214

SALARET
The situation has grown beyond me—sown with traps
and menaces for me as well as for you. There are
whisperings and rumblings and preparations of I don't
know what—and I don't want to know. I am tired
of the strain. Far better to leave this witches' cauldron
to seethe as it will. I have already sent my younger
children to Italy, where they are sure of food at least.
Come!

ESTER DA GRASSO
And let the Queen die deserted?

SALARET
Threatened Queens live long. Already her execution
has been postponed.

ESTER DA GRASSO
Only because Riffoni was called to quell the peasant
rising. But now that he is coming home—— O my
poor Margherita!
    [*Hurrying out hysterically.*]

SALARET [*Desperately*]
Stop, Armida! His return endangers only you.

ESTER DA GRASSO [*Turing incredulous*]
How only me?
Because I have been able to keep you alive so far
on the plea you were necessary to the Queen's last
hours. But now that she is not to be executed——

ESTER DA GRASSO
Not to be executed?

SALARET

No. I ought not to tell you these State secrets, but Riffoni found Western sentiment so outraged——

ESTER DA GRASSO [*Excitedly*]

We know from a New York paper Omar slipped in that an American petition was cabled to Riffoni.

SALARET

Quite so. And it impressed him particularly because it was got up by that same Nicholas Stone whose book we ran through the *Sera*. As, moreover, he desires commercial relations with the States, he decided to forgo her death.

ESTER DA GRASSO [*Bursting into tears*]

Thank God!

SALARET

So you see you have only to save yourself.

ESTER DA GRASSO

For what? I am not worth saving.

SALARET

Nonsense, pull yourself together, *cara*. The yacht lies moored near the Fort Prison—I can pretend I'm transferring you to your old cell—look!

    [*Opens the casement*]

You can see her funnels!

    [*From the Piazza comes up the rumble of waggons advancing, followed by raucous cries of a mob. "The Red Flag" begins to mingle with "The Marseillaise."*]

216

ESTER DA GRASSO
What's going on?
> [SHE *rushes on the balcony and looks down. Then
> she utters a scream, rushes back, bangs the casement
> to, and leans panting against it, as if to shut out
> what she has seen.*]

SALARET
What is it, Armida? What is the matter?

ESTER DA GRASSO [*Shrieking at him*]
Murderer!
> [HE *goes puzzled to the casement*]
Don't open it! They are bringing the guillotine!

SALARET [*Amazed*]
In broad daylight?

ESTER DA GRASSO
You lied to me—the execution is imminent.

SALARET [*Dully*]
Not before to-morrow morning.

ESTER DA GRASSO [*Wrings her jewelled hands*]
O blessèd Mother!

SALARET
I lied to you because it was the only way to save you.
Riffoni telegraphed instructions for both your deaths.
Unless you come at once——

ESTER DA GRASSO
Let me be! If only I can really help her last
moments——!

217

SALARET

I don't understand you, Armida. You were condemned for complicity in shooting down you land-hungry peasants. You were a frenzied proprietor, not a fanatical Royalist.

ESTER DA GRASSO

I am fanatical for the woman, not the Queen. I had never really known her. It was you who brought me under her spell. Why did you make me love her, if you only meant to butcher her?

SALARET

We are not butchering her—she had a fair trial.

ESTER DA GRASSO

And do you call that a trial in which, faced with the filthy insinuations of renegade courtiers, the poor angel refused to open her lips? And now your State cinemas display forged films of her amours with Fiuma and D'Azollo. I hear our guards sniggering over them—it is abominable.

SALARET

A little scandal goes a long way, I know. But Riffoni believes fervently in the Fiuma story at least.

ESTER DA GRASSO

Then it can only be to drug the dregs of his conscience.

SALARET

To drug his heart-ache, more likely. He feels her death necessary to the State, and if he did not think

218

her unworthy of his love, the conflict between passion
and duty would drive him mad.

ESTER DA GRASSO [*Amazed*]
He loves Margherita?

SALARET
She has not told you?

ESTER DA GRASSO
Not that. The heart that refused to open to the
Court has not been so closed to unworthy me. But
that the brute dared to desire her——no, she could not
bring her tongue to tell me that. As for liaisons of
her own——!
   [*Indignation and sobs choke her utterance.*]

SALARET
Anyhow she was not condemned for them, but for her
political crimes. She might have replied to those
charges at least.

ESTER DA GRASSO
Why should she stoop to justify herself, when life
had become indifferent to her?

SALARET
How you women evade! But if it's true she doesn't
want life, why do you want it for her?

ESTER DA GRASSO
Because the tragedy has deepened——she wants it desperately now.

SALARET
Aha!

ESTER DA GRASSO
Your masculine complacency is maddening. That
cabled petition from America seems to have unfrozen
her, and set her yearning to escape from the cockpit
of Europe, and settle incognita in those kindly States;
working at her music. I even gather there's a love
romance—some young attaché at our legation presumably, whom she would now be free to marry. Cazotti
seems to have told her he was married, but even she
has now begun to doubt Cazotti.

SALARET
Poor woman! I wish sincerely I could deposit her in
the young man's arms.

ESTER DA GRASSO [*Hysterically*]
Can't you? Can't you take her on the yacht?
    [*Embracing him frenziedly*]
I will love you so much, Rinaldo.

SALARET
Impossible, *cara*. Captain Lambri would cut off his
own nose rather than lose the Queen's head. He is
Redder even than Riffoni. He warned Cazotti, whom
he mistrusts, that in the event of a counter-revolution,
or even any attempted escape of the Queen, he would
stab her with his own hand.

ESTER DA GRASSO [*Recoiling, moaningly*]
How horrible! How horrible!
220

SALARET

Do not make it more horrible, Armida, by dying with her.

ESTER DA GRASSO

That is the only thing that could make it endurable.

SALARET

You are talking wildly. Think of our nights under the stars.

[*Tries to draw her to him again.*]

ESTER DA GRASSO [*Breaking away*]

I hate you. You told me when you took me that you had power of life and death. But it seems now it is Captain Lambri. Well, perhaps he is a man too—perhaps——

[*Exit frenziedly.*]

SALARET [*Dazedly, as she is disappearing*]

What do you mean? You are mad! . . . Stop!

[HE *rushes to the gong and strikes it repeatedly in his agitation.* VANNI *and the soldiers rush in*]

Arrest her.

VANNI

Who?

SALARET [*Sobered by the sight of them*]

Nobody.

[HE *pulls out his spectacles, cleans them nervously and puts them on*]

What I mean is, arrest the setting up of the guillotine. Telephone to Komak that——

221

VANNI [*Opening his eyes*]
But he is hanged————!

SALARET [*Shuddering*]
Yes, yes, my tongue slipped. Telephone to the new
Police Commissary that not even the platform must
be put up now. It must be done decently in the dead
of night.

VANNI
Into line, Comrades.
   [HE *salutes and goes out through the curtains.
   After a moment* SALARET *follows him, distractedly
   re-polishing his spectacles. In the first silent pause
   the confused songs and cries of the crowd are heard
   more loudly. A soldier, piqued by curiosity, opens
   the casement and steals out to look from the balcony. The sounds swell and other soldiers gradu-
   ally follow him, opening the other casement too.
   One distinguishes the commands of gendarmes, the
   calls of labourers moving timber, the brutal laughter of hooligans.* VANNI *returns to an empty
   stage*]
Hell and damnation!
   [HE *perceives the open casements*]
Come out of that, you swine! Never seen a guillotine
put up before?
   [*They slink in as he talks and close the casements
   behind them*]
Not that they'll trouble to put one up for you—a
lamppost does for the likes of us. Though, come to
think of it, if we're all equals and comrades, why
222

should the Queen die more handsomely than my brother-in-law?

GUARDS
Ha! ha! ha!

VANNI
That's not a joke, you sons of bitches. How dare you laugh at poor Fenella's bereavement! Cazotti the Compassionate did his best to save him, but you might as well talk to that mountain-top. And Stefano won't be the last to wear the poor man's necktie. It comes cheaper than Kites, eh? *They're* a nice spirited way of fighting, I must say, for a man who's ever sat a horse or spiked a Bosni. Poison-gas, indeed! If I had wanted to poison people, I'd have been a wine-seller, not a soldier. . . . Why the hell don't you laugh when you *do* hear a joke?

GUARDS [*Feebly*]
He! he! he!

VANNI
Cristo! It's neither grub nor glory for the soldier nowadays. Ah, they want to chop off *her* head now, but it wasn't like that, boys, when *She* sat there——
    [*Points to the throne*]
We got our knives into the Bosnis and our forks into the bacon.

GUARDS [*With beautiful unanimity*]
Ha! ha! ha!

223

VANNI [*Beaming*]
And when a filthy naturalised Bosni blew off my arm,
there was scarcely a day but the Queen came to the
hospital with chrysanthemums and jellies. Fancy Riffoni carrying a chap flowers!

GUARDS
Down with Riffoni!

VANNI
And God save the Queen!

GUARDS
God save the Queen!

CAZOTTI [*Who has come between the pillars unper-
ceived*]
Treason! Open treason in the People's Hall! What
does this mean, Corporal Vanni?

VANNI
I—your Excellency—Comrade——

CAZOTTI
Dismiss your men. You shall answer to me for this,
alone.

VANNI [*Confused*]
Right about turn, you swine. March!
[*Exeunt soldiers.*]

CAZOTTI
You indiscreet imbecile! For aught you knew I might
have been the President!

224

VANNI
But I should have heard the band returning, Excellency.

CAZOTTI
It happens he *is* coming with the procession. But he *might* have slipped home by car to evade assassins.
   [*A church-clock strikes the half-hour.* HE *lowers his voice*]
Fortunately the danger from your folly will soon be over. He dies to-day.

VANNI [*Startled*]
To-day?

CAZOTTI
Before that clock strikes the hour. How else can we save the Queen, God bless her?

VANNI
God bless her! When do I shoot Captain Lambri?

CAZOTTI
I have told you. Not till you hear a shot from this balcony.
   [*Points to the right casement*]
That will be the signal to Fenella's crowd that Riffoni is dead. Then you rush your men towards the Queen's apartments, while Fenella burts into the Palace.

VANNI
But I've been thinking, Excellency—won't that shot serve to warn Captain Lambri?

225

CAZOTTI
He'll hardly hear it where he is. Do give up thinking, Corporal, it doesn't suit a soldier, and you haven't Fenella's brains. Ah, I wish I could have saved her husband for her. But Riffoni was too rabid.

VANNI
A heart of stone, Excellency.

CAZOTTI
It will soon be cold as one.

VANNI
The saints be praised. And then we shall have enough grub again?

CAZOTTI [*Smiling*]
Tons. Though your men will no longer get the same rations as you.

VANNI [*Chuckling*]
I shan't tell 'em that.

CAZOTTI
For once you are sensible. Tell them as little as possible—just rush them about. But remember! no budging till you hear that shot from the balcony— instead of saving the Queen you might kill all of us, if you moved before the mob, or while Riffoni remained alive and kicking.

VANNI
I understand. But if he shouts for help or beats his gong?

CAZOTTI

If he beats it once, you march in as usual. But if he beats it twice, you're as deaf as *he* was to Stefano's cries for mercy. By the way, take no notice either of the shot that kills him—that will be point-blank and muffled by his damned brains.

[*Re-enter* SALARET *spectacled.*]

SALARET [*To* VANNI]

Did you tell the Commissary——? Ah, how do you do, Cazotti?

VANNI

The Commissary said, Excellency, that his guillotine carpenters won't work at night.

[*Salutes and exit.*]

SALARET

But surely, Cazotti, he could have waited till Riffoni had passed.

CAZOTTI

You saw Riffoni's wire forbidding further delay. And new brooms sweep clean.

SALARET

Clean? He has swept into the Piazza the rowdiest and basest elements.

CAZOTTI

So much the better for our *coup d'état.*

SALARET

It is for to-day?

227

CAZOTTI

To-morrow the trainload of food that Riffoni has brought home will allay the *stomach* for revolution. To-morrow those whose one hope is to save the Queen will have been disheartened. Ah, his haste to execute her has but precipitated his doom. Truly those whom the gods wish to destroy they first make mad. The bull was already made the last time he charged—do you remember how I shrugged my shoulder?—already I saw him dragged ignominiously from the arena. Bulls always charge with their eyes shut, and he failed to see that behind Stefano was Fenella, and behind Komak your Guido and the young generation. Had he consented to pardon them, I should have reaped only the profit of clemency, as it is, I reap the benefit of their deaths into the bargain.

SALARET

But the crowd seems as Red as Riffoni—didn't you hear its songs and screams?

CAZOTTI

My dear Salaret, crowds have no sentiments, sentiments have crowds. Fenella and her gang, aided by your son's pals among the Kite Corps, will, at the given signal, change the mood of the mob. The sight of the guillotine already evokes sympathy for the young Queen. Riffoni is hated even more than he is feared, and the mob is even hungrier than it is Republican and Socialist. And the moment they know Riffoni is dead, they will clamour for Cazotti the Compassionate.

228

SALARET [*Shocked*]
He is to die?

CAZOTTI
He will not survive his return by ten minutes.

SALARET
My God!

CAZOTTI
You *have* no God! What do you mean? Don't play
Salaret the Soft with me. Your friend chose to come
between me and the power I had worked for all my
life—he must be removed, he and his fantastic visions.

SALARET
But how will saving the Queen help *you* to the throne?

CAZOTTI
Who says the Queen will be saved? Captain Lambri
will look after that. Not that her death is necessary—
I would prefer to connive at her flight from the realm.
But Captain Lambri is impossible.

SALARET [*Hoarse and trembling*]
And who will—look after—Vittorio?

CAZOTTI
The person who has easiest access to him, of course.

SALARET [*Bounding*]
I?

CAZOTTI
As if I would rely on a reed! No——
    [*Lowering his voice with a chuckle*]

229

a man who would far rather shoot Lambri, if he guessed my combination.

[*Points to curtains.*]

SALARET
Omar? I thought he was whispering mischief. So he is a Royalist!

CAZOTTI
Yes.
[*Chuckling*]
That will cover us. Better still, he is an ex-servant of Gripstein. That will enable us to say, if necessary, that the Jews pulled the strings. Death is a strange glorifier and any reaction in Riffoni's favour will thus pass of harmlessly in a pogrom.

SALARET
I said you were the devil!

CAZOTTI [*Complacently*]
Of course there is also the danger of a reaction in the Queen's favour. But that is provided for by this letter I am sending to Riffoni the moment he returns.
[*Draws out from his breast-pocket an imposing sealed letter*]
It contains my resignation unless he accedes to the American petition and allows me to pardon the Queen —that will also put me right with America and the West generally.

SALARET
I wonder you tell me all this so nakedly, Cazotti.

CAZOTTI
Since my poor wife died I have no one to admire my combinations—or to call me by my Christian name. Won't you call me Alexis?

SALARET
When you are murdering the only man I do call by his Christian name! Are you not afraid I shall warn him?

CAZOTTI [*Patting his shoulder*]
I always said you were not dangerous. You know that you will breathe more freely when death snaps your schoolmaster and his cane.

SALARET [*With a sudden hope or fear, he scarcely knows which*]
But there is one piece on the chess-board you have overlooked—the protecting knight.

CAZOTTI
Molp? That man is a mystery. As devoted at heart to the Queen as Omar, he remains ferociously faithful to Riffoni. However a telegram has already met him at the station summoning him to the deathbed of his little Nina at her grandmother's in the country. . . .
    [*Laughing merrily at the mixture of horror and admiration on the face of his silenced colleague, he points to the throne*]
Would you mind taking the chair a moment?

SALARET
What for?

231

CAZOTTI

To witness the climax of the combination.

> [*Laughingly pushes the wondering* SALARET *into the royal chair and rings the bell. Enter* OMAR. CAZOTTI *hands him the letter*]

Here is the letter, Omar, and here

> [*Pointing to* SALARET]

is the President back—we will suppose. Now go out and let us see your conception of the part.

> [OMAR *grins, salaams and exit.*]

SALARET

What are we doing?

CAZOTTI

He is coming back to present my ultimatum to Riffoni, you being Riffoni.

SALARET

I being Riffoni?

CAZOTTI

How slow you are! The star part! Be very busy with these accumulations. But don't open the letter when Omar brings it—else I should have to write a new envelope. Just pretend to read it. You will naturally be perturbed at my threatened resignation. That will be Omar's opportunity.

SALARET

It is a rehearsal of the—— O my God!

CAZOTTI
Your God again! Omar has really an Allah, yet you
see he doesn't turn a hair. Atheists should be at least
as godless as believers.

SALARET
I am not an atheist in your sense. There is no God,
but a divine sap rises within us.

CAZOTTI [*With a coarse laugh*]
Tell that to Armida.

SALARET
I know I have sinned against my light. But to
implicate me in a murder——!
    [*Springs up.*]

CAZOTTI [*Pressing him back*]
Sit down.

SALARET
I told you I wouldn't have him murdered. . . . Your
colleague! What will the world think of you?

CAZOTTI
How dull you are to-day! The letter found on your
body—on *his* body, don't look so frightened—will not
only seal the legend of Cazotti the Compassionate, but
acquit me of any ambition to supplant either my
Queen or my President.

SALARET
But posterity will surely discover——

233

CAZOTTI
Posterity may say what it likes so long as it waits till
I am dead. Now do try to look the part—attend to
these accumulations.

SALARET [*Rising again*]
Don't torture me! Let Omar rehearse on *you*, if
rehearsal is necessary.

CAZOTTI
I have to be at the wing, giving Vanni his cue.

SALARET
Then why doesn't Omar come in and get it over?

CAZOTTI
My fault. The stage directions are he is not to enter
till Riffoni is alone. It is a scene constructed for two
characters only: any additional personage might
upset the tragedy.
        [*Pressing him back on the throne*]
Now I will leave the stage clear.
        [*Goes out smilingly through the pillars. An instant
        after* OMAR *enters by the curtains, with the letter on
        a salver.*]

OMAR
An immediate answer is requested, Effendi.
        [SALARET *pretends to open and read the letter,
        though his hands tremble violently.* OMAR *drops
        the salver, whips out a pistol and claps it to his
        forehead, with a mock cry*]
Bang!

[*Highly amused, he rushes with his pistol to the right casement, flings it open and leaps on to the balcony. Over the buzz of the crowd he utters a second mock cry*]

Bang!

CAZOTTI [*Without*]
Riffoni is dead! *Viva* Margherita! Yes, the bang was your cue, Vanni.

[HE *comes in, clapping his hands, as* OMAR *reappears from the balcony, closing the casement*]
Bravo, Omar, *Bravissimo*.

[*To* SALARET]
But I can't applaud *you*. Why didn't you fall? . . . Wait, Omar, you have forgotten the letter.

[OMAR, *grinning more broadly than ever, picks up the salver and letter and retires salaaming.* SALARET *collapses half-fainting, huddled on his chair.*]

CAZOTTI
Ah, if you had only done that at the right moment!

SALARET [*Springing up fiercely*]
Let me be! You might have spared me the dreadful foreknowledge.

CAZOTTI
I wanted you to know so as to keep out of the way. Go over to your yacht—it will be your safest position from every point of view.

SALARET
And where will you be?

CAZOTTI

In the Tower Room—another of my combinations—
for it combines freedom from risk with a fine view of
the counter-revolution. . . . Good-bye—I counsel you
to be off at once. Omar's revolver has six chambers
you heard, and fanatics don't like interference.

SALARET

Poor Omar! Working for you, though he thinks he is
working for his Queen.

CAZOTTI

Don't we all work to ends unseen? Even I may never
get to the throne—the greasy plank may give me a
tumble at the last inch—ah, your eyes light up at the
prospect. Do not deny it.

SALARET

I can't pretend that your restoring Monarchy and
Capitalism enraptures me. So this is the end of the
Revolution.

CAZOTTI

Isn't it the end of every Revolution—the top of the
wheel come round again? But who knows? Bis-
marck toyed with the idea of a monarchist Socialism,
and perhaps we statesman who have pandered to
democracy ought to be grateful to you for showing
that the State may be an apiary. But, alas! I fear
Socialism presupposes a quality which is not in human
nature.

SALARET
But *Riffoni* was honest.

CAZOTTI
Ha! ha! ha! I wasn't thinking of honesty but of omniscience—we are not as high above men as bee-masters above the hive, not even your Riffoni.
[HE *goes towards the curtains.*]

SALARET [*In a last desperate appeal*]
But Cazotti—Alexis!—is his death absolutely necessary?

CAZOTTI
Absolutely necessary. And absolutely deserved.

SALARET
Because he has killed others?

CAZOTTI
What an idea! Statesmen, like generals, cannot regard life. No, Riffoni must die like all men who adventure in waters too deep for them. He called up forces he cannot control, nourished illusions he cannot maintain, and raised expectations he cannot satisfy. He appealed to man's master-passion, Greed——

SALARET [*Fiercely*]
He appealed to man's master-passion, Justice!

CAZOTTI
Pooh! The sense of justice lives only because each man thinks *he* hasn't got his deserts.
[*Smiling*]
I don't suppose I shall be satisfied even as King.

237

SALARET [*Bitterly*]
No. Not if, as you say, the dose must always be increased. You will be wanting next to be Emperor of Europe.

CAZOTTI
Why not? It's the only way to turn the Cockpit into a Concert Hall.
[*Parts the curtains*]
Be off to your yacht!
[*Exit.*]

SALARET [*Miserably*]
My yacht!
[HE *opens the casement and gazes out. Above the buzz of the crowd comes the thump, thump of hammers.*]

VOICE [*From Piazza*]
Bring the cross-piece, you idiots! . . . No! No! The cross-piece!
[SALARET *shudders and closes the casement.* MOLP *in uniform and spurred comes in agitatedly through the pillars.* SALARET *turns, startled at the sight of him.*]

SALARET
You *here!*

MOLP [*Suspiciously*]
Where else should I be?

SALARET [*Recovering composure*]
In—in the procession.

MOLP
I galloped ahead to caution Vạnni and Omar.

SALARET
What about?

MOLP
Guarding the President. My little Nina is terribly ill,
dying perhaps.

SALARET
How sad! And such a journey for you!

MOLP [*Swiftly*]
How did you know it was a journey?

SALARET
You—you told me that having to accompany the
President on his campaign, you had to leave her at
her grandmother's.

MOLP
Did I? I thought it was Cazotti I told.
    [*Rings the bell*]
Suppose the wire from her village is a ruse?

SALARET
A ruse?

MOLP
I know my Valdania. I have practised too many tricks
239

myself. Suppose there was a plot against the President and they wanted to lure me away?

[*Enter* OMAR, *who is obviously startled to see him, but swiftly exchanges his surprise for an Oriental impassivity*]

Omar, I have an uneasy feeling a last attempt may be made to save the Queen. Let no stranger approach the President.

OMAR
No stranger shall approach.

MOLP
Swear it to me.

OMAR [*With convincing solemnity*]
By the beard of the Prophet, I swear it.

MOLP
And I swear by the tail of the devil that if anything happens to him, *you* shall pay the forfeit.

OMAR
It will be just.

MOLP
Good. *Addio*, Comrade Salaret.

SALARET [*Uneasily*]
Must you go?

MOLP
How can I stay away?

240

SALARET

But—but there seems such a savage crowd round the Palace. Listen!

[HE *throws open the blazoned casement. The command of a master-carpenter is heard above the noise and the hammering.*]

MASTER-CARPENTER [*Without*]

Fix in the knife, you fools, fix in the knife!

MOLP

Close it, close it, I know. I came through the mob—it's only what executions always draw. God spares me from the sight of that death at least.

[*Going towards the pillars.*]

SALARET [*Making talk to detain him*]

You were in her service, were you not?

MOLP

She could not bear the sight of me, but to me the sight of her was like an almond tree in the spring.

SALARET

Ah, that must have been in her own springtide.

MOLP

And now, so early, winter is upon her. Poor Margherita! How dreadful that her death is necessary to the Republic!

SALARET

Is it necessary?

241

MOLP

Absolutely necessary and absolutely deserved—the President has convinced me.

SALARET

Absolutely necessary and absolutely deserved. . . . Ha! ha! ha!

MOLP

What are you laughing at? Isn't he right?

SALARET

I suppose so. My friend Riffoni is a great man.

MOLP

The greatest I have ever known.

SALARET [*Rather surprised*]

Indeed? . . . Greater than Cazotti?

MOLP

Ah, they are the two creatures of our national arms, the serpent and the eagle.

SALARET [*Points to the blazoned throne*]

Yes, but look! It is the serpent that encircles the eagle.

MOLP

God save us!
    [*Crosses himself*]
So it is.
    [*Looks at watch*]
But I must catch my train.
    [*Moves on.*]

SALARET
Wait a moment!

MOLP
I can't—God help me.
  [*With a half-sob he goes out hurriedly.*]

SALARET [*Calling after him*]
Cheer up! I'm sure you'll find the child better.
  [HE *drops exhausted and trembling on a chair.
  After an instant* RIFFONI *comes quietly through the
  curtains in general's uniform, with spurs.* SALARET
  springs up, startled.]

RIFFONI [*Laughing*]
You look as if I were a ghost! What's the matter?
  [*Embraces him.*]

SALARET
I expected you to come with bands and banners.

RIFFONI
I came by the subway. I slipped out of the procession, when I found it would have to pass the
guillotine.

SALARET
I am glad it spoiled your triumph. Why, to-morrow
morning? Why such brutal haste?

RIFFONI [*Turns away to ascend dais*]
I was afraid if I saw her again I might waver.
243

SALARET
Yes, seeing people again makes a great difference.
You *ought* to have seen her again.

RIFFONI
Do not scold me, dear Master, I am very tired. Ah,
there is my old armchair.
    [*Drops on the throne*]
What was it Catullus said about the wanderer dropping
into his familiar seat?

SALARET
Catullus hardly had a throne in mind.

RIFFONI
Nor such a heap of correspondence.
    [*Takes up letters.*]

SALARET [*Alarmed*]
Must you attend to it now? Let's go for one of our
old walks and talks.

RIFFONI
When I am just in my armchair?
    [*Opens a letter*]
By the way, Molp's child is dangerously ill.

SALARET
I know. He looked in for a moment to admonish
Omar and Vanni to super-vigilance.

RIFFONI
Dear Molp! He has assassination on the brain. Ah,
244

I mustn't forget my promise to him to keep my pistol handy.

[*Lays it on the table*]

I do hope he'll find his Nina better. How vast it can be—the death of one child. I remember the spacious emptiness at home when my little brother was drowned. Poor Carlo with his long curls and his passion for paper-boats. Now the passing of myriads seems like the melting of bubbles.

[*The military music of the returning soldiers is heard faintly.*]

SALARET

Had you to sacrifice many peasants?

RIFFONI

I spared as many as I could. But I had to think of our foodless cities, and our imperilled social structure. Ah, the ancients symbolised profoundly when they laid human sacrifices in the basement of their buildings. But for how long, I ask myself, will our house stand unshaken, for how long will there be food in its larder? The unrest seems too deep-seated, one might as well try to extinguish a volcano with a fire-hose. Ah, as I mowed down the poor stupid peasants, who could not understand that the crops must be communised as well as the land, the Queen's words kept rising up against me—yes, even the Duke's—and I wondered—forgive me, dear Master—whether the Workers' Republic was indeed only a forcing house. Perhaps mankind runs to property as the male chin to hair. Can we breed a beardless sex by the razor?

245

SALARET

Or ensure a Republic by the guillotine?

RIFFONI

Do not raise that question—I am unhappy enough.
  [*The soldiers swing buoyantly past to their music*]
Ha! Do you hear? She talks to me of love and
pity and that was her own music—her own war-march
against Bosnavina. Fate has made it her death-march.
  [OMAR *parts the curtains, holding the* CAZOTTI
  letter on a salver, but, obviously disconcerted by
  SALARET'S *presence, he withdraws, unmarked save
  of* SALARET]
And yet that vivid flame blown out, that flesh so soft
and warm to fatten worms—what madness is this?

SALARET

Ah, you love her! You love her still!

RIFFONI

No, no, who could love the creature the trial revealed?

SALARET

Even were it all true, would she be less desirable?
Molp just said that in her springtide she was lovely
as almond-blossom. Suffering has dulled that rosy
radiance, but give her freedom and happiness and you
will enjoy her re-flowering.

RIFFONI

I shall enjoy? But she shrinks from my touch.

246

SALARET

That was her guile, you said. Get her at close quarters—you will soon learn if you are less attractive than the others.

RIFFONI

At close quarters?

SALARET

Carry her off to the Mediterranean, to some enchanted island. You say you are very tired. Leave all this cumber before your nerves break down. Try a dose of joy.

RIFFONI

Your love for me unbalances you—you forget she dies to-morrow.

SALARET

Take her to-night then. Luckily my yacht is provisioned and coaled and can sail at a moment's notice.

RIFFONI

Eh? How comes that?

SALARET

I—I decided to take a holiday when you returned—the strain without you was too great. The moment your wire came. I made arrangements. Come *with* me.

RIFFONI

It is too sudden.

247

SALARET

Your bag is not yet unpacked. All we need is to
manœuvre the Queen on board——
[*Gives him a pen*]
Write me an order for Captain Lambri to hand her
over to my charge for secret removal to the Fort
Prison, on the ground of a possible Royalist attempt
at rescue this last night. I will persuade her lady-in-
waiting that I am helping them to escape your clutches.
They won't dream you are on board till the yacht has
sailed. Come! You must slip away at once.

RIFFONI [*Momentarily carried away*]

Where is the yacht?

SALARET

Moored near the Fort. Look! You can just see her
funnels.
[*Opens the blazoned casement.* RIFFONI *descends
from his throne.*]

RIFFONI [*Looking*]

But why this lightning speed?
[*The sinister sound of hammers beats up from the
Piazza.*]

SALARET [*Shuddering and closing casement*]

There is your answer.

RIFFONI

But I could reprieve her for a day or two.

248

SALARET
And suffer again all the agonies of indecision and
desire, the more agonising because your nature is
action? Come, obey the law of your being!

RIFFONI
And to-morrow morning—how do we explain her
absence?

SALARET
Obviously on the ground that the Royalist rescue we
apprehended was effected during the transference.

RIFFONI
Humph.   Highly   ingenious   for   an   academic
philosopher. But obey the law of *your* being, Salaret,
and do not outrage your sense of right in your over-
solicitude for my happiness. Why, when I merely
grasped her hand in this very room, you rightly
restrained me; why do you egg me on to violence now?

SALARET
Who spoke of violence? Opportunity, which makes
the thief, favours also the lover. You could woo her
at your leisure.

RIFFONI
Leisure! My work gives me none.
    [*Re-seats himself and takes up a letter.*]

SALARET [*Desperate, burning his boats*]
Your work? Pouring water down volcanoes!
249

RIFFONI
I said that in a moment of weariness.

SALARET
In a moment of insight.   Our Republic is an abortion.

RIFFONI
You believe that!   *You!*   All our painful parturition——?

SALARET
Worse than wasted.   If only I could get you away, give you a little happiness.

RIFFONI
I never sought happiness.

SALARET
It seeks you.

RIFFONI
It must find me at my post.

SALARET
That post need not be Valdania.

RIFFONI
How do you mean?

SALARET
It is an impossible country; illiterate, priest-ridden, rooted immovably in the dead past.   A new idea needs a new world.   Let us sail to some more plastic country —Paraguay, perhaps, the scene of so many social

experiments, whence we could get a leverage over all South America, the continent of the future.

RIFFONI
It is a great conception—like all yours. Unfortunately, as Gripstein pointed out to me, when I went to him about the *Sera,* you can't overturn Capitalism without capital.

SALARET
But there is gold on the yacht—masses.

RIFFONI
On board? How?

SALARET
Isn't it a State yacht? I store the Treasury bullion there. In these turbulent times it is best to keep the whereabouts of our gold unknown.

RIFFONI [*Smiling*]
So Gripstein thought. But we can't carry off Valdania's finances.

SALARET
You talk like a bourgeois. Since we shall devote them to our ideal——!
    [*Enter* ESTER DA GRASSO, *with* OMAR *protesting.*]

ESTER DA GRASSO [*Frantically pushing past* OMAR]
Stand aside!
    [OMAR *disappears*]
O Signor Riffoni, be merciful. I do not ask you to
251

stop the execution. But stop that hammering, for God's sake, or remove Her Majesty to a room which does not give on the Piazza. I have kept her from the window, I have already pulled down the blind and closed the shutters, I have tried to drown the sounds with her own music. But underneath, I know she has divined, that every stroke of the hammer beats on her heart. Ah, she is so young, so young———!

[*Sobs.*]

SALARET
Calm yourself, Signora. We will remove her from the Palace altogether—to the Fort Prison.

ESTER DA GRASSO
Ah, yes, yes, my old quarters—that will be quiet, and free from this ghoulish mob.

SALARET [*Writing*]
The President will sign this order to Captain Lambri. Bring her to me, dressed for the transference, with her things for the night. You will accompany her, of course.

[HE *gives the paper to* RIFFONI, *who, hypnotised, signs it.* SALARET *hands it to* ESTER DA GRASSO.]

ESTER DA GRASSO
God bless you both for this mercy at least!

[*Exit as she came.*]

SALARET
Wasn't that providential—if I may use the word?

RIFFONI [*Rapt*]
And I shall see her again!

SALARET
Day after day——come, let us get your bag. My car
is at the gate.

RIFFONI
She will not smile, I fear. Only once did I see her
smile. It was like the spreading of sunshine over a
crystal pool.

SALARET
As soon as you reach the yacht, send the car back for
us. It is not three minutes by the short cuts.

RIFFONI
Ah no——they can't be true, those stories——with that
smile!

SALARET
I will bring her to the yacht with her Dame of Honour.
    [*Takes his arm to get him to move.*]

RIFFONI
But she is coming here, you said——I shall see her at
once.

SALARET
No, no——you might be indiscreet——she might smell a
rat.

253

RIFFONI
I shall speak only of the Fort Prison—I shall not
mention the yacht. You shall take them on board and
send the car back for me.

SALARET
No—you must be on board first—surely you can wait
ten minutes.

RIFFONI
And if your tyre burst in bringing her—no, no, I have
starved long enough!
　　[*Enter* OMAR.]

OMAR
Signora da Grasso begs that Signor Salaret will come
to her at once.

SALARET
Ha!
　　[OMAR *salaams and exit.*]

RIFFONI [*Feverishly*]
Is it a hitch? Does the Queen cling to her room after
all?

SALARET
Who can say? Women are so unexpected. Or perhaps
it's that ferocious Captain Lambri refusing to let them
go.
　　[*Hurries out.*]

254

RIFFONI
The insolent dog! Put him in his place! . . . To
watch her re-flowering——
    [HE *muses ecstatically. The curtains part and*
    OMAR *appears with the big heavily-sealed letter on*
    the salver]
What is it?

OMAR
An immediate answer is requested, Effendi.

RIFFONI
Put it down—I can't attend to it now.

OMAR
But it is from Comrade Cazotti, Effendi. I dare not
return, empty-handed.

RIFFONI
The devil take you both!
    [HE *opens the letter.* OMAR'S *hand slides to his*
    bosom. MOLP *enters through the pillars*]
Ah, you're back! You've had reassuring news?

MOLP
No, but I could not bring myself to catch my train—I
was haunted by a vision.

RIFFONI
Indeed? Of what?

MOLP
Of a serpent encircling an eagle.

255

RIFFONI
The arms of Valdania? Why should that keep you
from little Nina?

MOLP
I was reminded of my duty to protect Valdania's
President.

RIFFONI [*Deeply touched*]
You put your duty to me before your love for your
child?

MOLP
Not entirely. I wasn't sure the telegram wasn't a
ruse.

RIFFONI [*Huskily*]
Don't whittle it down—you are a quixotic idiot. Get
a car and be off at once.

MOLP
With all respect, now I must wait for the reply to my
telegram of enquiry.

RIFFONI [*Facetiously covering his emotion*]
That's not so idiotic.
    [*Looks at letter*]
Ha! ha! ha! How odd! Why didn't he say so
before? Cazotti threatens resignation unless I allow
him to pardon the Queen. . . . What would you have
me reply?
    [*Takes up pen and paper.*]

MOLP
The eagle does not take counsel of the sparrow.

RIFFONI
Don't talk like our friend here. What would *you* like
me to do?

MOLP
You will always do what the welfare of the Republic
demands.

RIFFONI [*Touched and troubled*]
Will I, indeed? Ah, if you knew how nearly the
serpent had dragged down the eagle! Answer my
question—what would *you* do if only *your* welfare was
concerned?

MOLP
Sooner than hurt a hair of her head I would go to the
block myself.

RIFFONI
Brave Molp! . . . I am sorry the welfare of the
Republic demands my acceptance of the resignation.
    [*Writes and gives the answer to* OMAR, *who salaams
    stoically and exit*]
Don't look so gloomy, Molp. Who is Cazotti to
pardon an angel?

MOLP [*Ecstatic*]
You will pardon her yourself?

RIFFONI
Not even I am worthy. She will escape.

257

MOLP
Escape? By your connivance?

RIFFONI
And yours.

MOLP
Thank God! Ah, how great you are!

RIFFONI
Tut! Tut! *You* are the big man. We are pre-
tending to transfer her to the Fort Prison with her
lady-in-waiting, but in reality we shall put them on
board Salaret's yacht. He is worn out, poor man, and
sees the Republic not in red but in black. A sea
voyage will pick him up, give him fresh faith.

MOLP
He will sail down the river then?

RIFFONI
Yes, into the Mediterranean. And land the Queen at
any port she chooses.
    [*Re-enter* SALARET *frenziedly.*]

SALARET [*In wild relief*]
Ah, you are alive! And Molp is back! Splendid!

RIFFONI
What are you maundering about? What did she
want? You may speak before Molp.
258

SALARET

I didn't see them—they were dressing—Omar must have—er—misunderstood. Captain Lambri is bringing them.

RIFFONI

Good. I was just going to explain to Molp that I want *him* to act as escort—it will be less suspicious—and then he can return, wounded.

MOLP [*Startled*]

Eh?

RIFFONI [*Smiling*]

Bandaged, anyhow—you said you would go to the block for her. You will explain that a party of Royalists attacked you and carried off the Queen to the mountains.

SALARET

A false track—an admirable addition!

MOLP

It won't look very plausible entrusting her to a single escort.

RIFFONI

Why not? If our idea was to keep her removal unobserved. Do motor down at once, Salaret, and instruct the captain to get up steam. Then return at top speed and wait at the gate till Molp brings down the ladies.

259

SALARET
But you?

RIFFONI
Quick! I hear them coming.

> [*Bundles the semi-dazed* SALARET *out between the pillars, while the* QUEEN *and* ESTER DA GRASSO *in travelling attire, the latter carrying a little bag, enter the opposite way, with* CAPTAIN LAMBRI *in their wake; a truculent officer with a fierce moustache, who salutes the President, clicking his heels*]

I thank you Comrade Lambri for your vigilance. Colonel Molp will see to the transference of your prisoners. Molp, will you have the courtesy to relieve the Signora of that bag?

> [LAMBRI *glares ferociously as* MOLP *takes it*]

Of course, Captain Lambri, we must not attract Royalist attention to the Queen's removal. But as soon as it is quite dark, please station your company outside the Fort Prison.

> [CAPTAIN LAMBRI, *pacified, salutes and goes.*]

QUEEN
I am grateful to you, Signor Riffoni, for your consideration.

RIFFONI
I sincerely regret it is the last I can show you.

ESTER DA GRASSO [*Hysterically*]
But why can't you spare her? I know they cabled you from America to pardon her.

QUEEN
Hush, dear Ester! You haven't fastened your brooch
—it will fall out.
    [*Fastens it for her with fingers that do not falter*]
Signor Riffoni must follow his sense of his Republic's
necessities.

RIFFONI
I thank you, Madam. You as a ruler have learnt that
one cannot always please oneself. To pardon you
would set Captain Lambri's faction raging—more
bloodshed might ensue. But I have just instructed
Colonel Molp—by the way, that bag is surely too
small——

QUEEN
It is only for one night.

RIFFONI
Ah, well, I expect you can pick up more *en route*.

QUEEN [*Almost breaking down for the first time*]
Ah, do not put it off any longer. That would be the
cruellest kindness.

ESTER DA GRASSO
Yes, kill her—you shall not torture her any longer!

RIFFONI
But it is the end of her torture, I am trying to tell you.
    [*To* QUEEN]
It is to freedom, Madam, that Comrade Molp will
escort you.

261

ESTER DA GRASSO [*Ceasing to sob*]
To freedom?

QUEEN [*With her first sob*]
To freedom?

RIFFONI [*Smiling, to hide his own emotion*]
Only—don't let the cat out of that bag—you must
tell your friends you were rescued by a Royalist raid.

QUEEN [*Dazed*]
I am free to go where I please?

RIFFONI
Where you please.   Even to America.

QUEEN
Oh!
    [*Breaks down and covers her eyes.*]

RIFFONI
I must risk your raising opinion against us.

QUEEN
But—Signor Riffoni—my only ambition is to sink
quietly into the Melting Pot.

ESTER DA GRASSO
And marry an American.

QUEEN [*Blushing*]
Ester——!

262

RIFFONI [*Huskily*]
So much the better. . . .
   [*Clearing his throat*]
Now, Molp, march!

QUEEN
Addio then.   How can I thank you?
   [SHE *offers him her hand.*]

RIFFONI
You would touch my hand?

QUEEN
It is stained with blood, but not—I feel—with dis-
honour.

RIFFONI
Ah, Madam!
   [HE *bends and kisses her hand*]
The pioneer's hand can never be clean, and we who
create civilisation are like the swine-grease through
which perfumes are distilled for the delicate nostril.
But, in so far as is practicable, I will try to work in
your spirit.

QUEEN
In your father's spirit, Signor Vittorio.

RIFFONI
Put it as you please—I shall always feel you are the
Lady of our Republic.
263

QUEEN

God grant you may remember. . . . We are ready,
Colonel Molp. Ah, God forgive my selfishness! The
Duke? What of him?

RIFFONI

D'Azollo?
 [*Laughs boisterously to relieve his emotion*]
Ah, it is wonderful how he always goes out of my head.
Talk of *his* memory!
 [*Starts writing*]
Of course you shall have your Duke—the Royalist
raid will capture quite a bag, eh, Molp? Larger than
that! Ha! ha! ha!

QUEEN

God bless you.

RIFFONI [*Handing the order to* MOLP]

Bless Molp—it is all his doing.
 [*To the astonished* MOLP]
No, I know you don't understand; you wouldn't be
Molp if you did. Do you remember the Duke asking
me that night what I would do with his yacht? Won't
he be amused at my putting him on it!

ESTER DA GRASSO

The Duke's yacht?

RIFFONI

Salaret's now, more or less—it is *that* you are to escape
on.

264

ESTER DA GRASSO
With Salaret on board?

RIFFONI [*Genially*]
Oh, yes, you shall have the Professor to see you
through. Colonel Molp, unfortunately, cannot leave
Valdania. His little girl is dangerously ill.

ESTER DA GRASSO
O my God! No, no, kill her rather. . . . O blessèd
Virgin!

RIFFONI
Kill the child? What can you mean?

ESTER DA GRASSO
It is a trap!
    [*Tugs at the* QUEEN's *cloak*]
Come back, Your Majesty. Ah, I thought it was too
good to be true.

QUEEN
What trap? What are you in fever about? . . . Poor
little Nina! I am so sorry, Colonel——

ESTER DA GRASSO
Ah, I ought to have understood earlier—when the
Fort Prison cropped up again.
[*Turns on* RIFFONI]
O you unspeakable——!

QUEEN
Ester! Compose yourself! I don't understand you.
265

ESTER DA GRASSO
No, Your Majesty, you never did. I should have
confessed everything earlier, God forgive me. All my
life I have had lovers—ah, I knew you would shrink
from me. But better that you should shrink from me
than rush into that! Is it so disgraceful to give oneself when the heart is free to open or close? I did
not think so till your innocence came like a rebuke—
there was always romance to redeem. But here—
through dread of the thorns, I whose life had been all
roses—through a cowardly fear of pain and death, I
have sunk to my gaoler!
[*Breaks down, hides her face.*]

RIFFONI
To your gaoler? Which gaoler?

ESTER DA GRASSO
As if you did not know!

RIFFONI
But I know nothing.

ESTER DA GRASSO
So I was led to believe. But now I see that the devilish
sense of power has wrought on you likewise. Only
you flew at higher game and bided your time. Come
back, Margherita, that hammering is less dreadful.

RIFFONI
Stay, Signora. You cannot go, leaving such imputa-
tions. Do I understand that you are afraid that if the
Queen goes on board the yacht——?

266

ESTER DA GRASSO
She will find *you* there—as I shall find Salaret. O,
I could endure these orgies myself if it would really
save *her*. But that she too——!

RIFFONI
These orgies?

ESTER DA GRASSO
It was only towards the end of the cruise that Salaret
discovered I was his special affinity.

RIFFONI
Salaret? . . . You are raving!

ESTER DA GRASSO
Alas, my sanity has stood the shock.

RIFFONI
Molp, do you know anything of this?

MOLP
It was before my time. But I did suspect something
lately between Salaret and the Signora.

ESTER DA GRASSO
But I only let him in once—the first night—ah, you
can never forgive me, Madam.

QUEEN
I forgive you now, Ester. You have saved me from
worse than death.
    [ESTER *falls sobbing into her arms*]

Hush! We must go back. Give me the bag, Colonel
Molp!

[MOLP *hesitates. In the tense silence the banging of
the hammers penetrates again.*]

RIFFONI
Do nothing of the sort, Molp! Ah, Madam, your
friend would destroy, not save you. Go in tranquillity;
we need the guillotine for a real criminal. I wish I
could utterly deny the devilish design you attribute to
me, but it had been exorcised—by this brave Comrade
—even before your horror had brought home to me its
full baseness. I had resolved to seek oblivion of you
and purgation of myself in my work for the Republic.
. . . Ah, how can I believe in the Republic now?
[*Sinks broken into his throne*]
Go, Comrade. Salaret should be waiting in his car by
the time you get to the gate. Send him up to me and
drive off at once with the ladies, and let the captain
cast anchor immediately. Then they will be sure
Salaret is not on board—nor I.

QUEEN
Come, Ester.

ESTER DA GRASSO
No, no! He is play-acting. What is to prevent him
coming on board afterwards? I would not trust him
on his oath.

RIFFONI
You must trust me without it, Signora, for God in
heaven I have none.

268

MOLP

But *I* have, by God, and I swear I will never leave Her
Majesty till she is safe among her friends!

RIFFONI

But your Nina——!

MOLP

She must live or die without me.
> [ESTER DA GRASSO *looks at* MOLP, *then takes the*
> QUEEN'S *hand and moves towards the pillars.*]

MOLP

Excuse my preceding Your Majesty—I have to show
the pass.
> [*Exit; they follow.*]

RIFFONI [*Hurrying down from the dais*]
One moment, Madam! Accept a parting gift.

QUEEN [*Moving a few steps within*]
Your pistol?

RIFFONI
Loaded. Your final safeguard.

QUEEN [*Taking it*]
To think that I came to this Palace with love in my
heart and go with death in my hand.

RIFFONI
I trust at least you go to happiness.

QUEEN

It is a happiness merely to go—to be released by
God . . . to feel my forehead finally free of the
crown. . . .

> [*With sudden gaiety* SHE *curtseys to the empty
> throne*]

Good-bye, you!

> [*Exit.*]

RIFFONI

Ah, she is younger already—she will flower again. . . .

> [*Calls after her*]

But the Duke! Don't forget to collect the Duke!
Aha, I remembered him at last. Ha! ha! ha! ha! ha!

> [*Mounts the dais in hysteric, half-sobbing laughter,
> and, dropping on his throne, rings the bell. Enter*
> OMAR.]

RIFFONI

Give me your pistol, Omar.

OMAR [*Utterly disconcerted*]

Effendi!

RIFFONI

You carry a pistol for my protection, do you not?

> [OMAR *nods, speechless for once*]

Give it me!

> [*Hypnotised,* OMAR *slowly hands it over.*]

RIFFONI

It is loaded?

270

OMAR
In every chamber.

RIFFONI
Good. . . . I have parted with mine. You may go!
. . . By the way, you gave my reply to Comrade
Cazotti?

OMAR
Yes, Effendi.

RIFFONI
Did he say anything?

OMAR
Not to your humble servant.
[*Salaams and exit.* RIFFONI *examines the pistol
in a silence through which the hammering is heard
again. Enter* SALARET *by the pillars.*]

RIFFONI [*Sardonically, playing with the pistol*]
Ah, Salaret, all going well?

SALARET
To perfection. Steam is up and the car gone off. We
have only to follow secretly. But I was surprised to
see the Duke in the party—is that wise? Won't he
put a spoke in our wheel?

RIFFONI [*With ferocious gaiety*]
In *his* wheel, Salaret. Isn't the yacht his?

SALARET
Ah, you are gay at last.

271

RIFFONI [*With savage blandness*]
Thanks to my wise Master. . . . So in five minutes
we shall be off to El Dorado!

SALARET
We carry El Dorado with us, ha! ha! ha!

RIFFONI
Ah, the gold, you mean. I had forgotten that . . .
[*Smiling*]
Suppose the Duke should claim it?

SALARET
I said he would interfere.

RIFFONI
Interfere with your Department! Not while you're
alive, I promise you.

SALARET [*Grumblingly*]
Your weakness for the Duke will yet cost you dear.

RIFFONI
But not as dear as all that, Salaret. There are
millions, eh? Enough to turn Paraguay into a
Workers' Paradise!

SALARET
Trust me. Cazotti won't be so pleased to be Finance
Minister now.

RIFFONI
Ah, that sticks in your gizzard, does it? But if
Paraguay prove recalcitrant?

SALARET
The world is wide.

RIFFONI
Yes, all those far-stretching seas and continents—and
yet it could all be dropped down a rift in the sun and
lost like a little green bead.   And the sun itself could
be sucked up into Sirius like my little brother into the
lake, with scarcely a ripple.   What do you suppose
this measureless mass of mud we call the universe is
in such a whirl for, Salaret?

SALARET
For love and joy, Vittorio.   Remember Goethe.   Dry
and dead is all theory, green and beautiful is living.
Wait!   Wait!   You will soon cease to ask questions
of the universe.

RIFFONI
You mean, if the Queen — but suppose she proves
marble-cold?   Do you think Signora da Grasso——?

SALARET
Oh, but I am sure the Queen won't resist you.   And
you don't like Signora da Grasso, you said.

RIFFONI
I said she reeked with sex.   And so should I by that
time—shouldn't I?   The tiger, they say, once it has
tasted blood rarely returns to a milk diet.

SALARET [*Perturbed*]
But Signora da Grasso is not the only lady still un-
executed.

273

RIFFONI
Ah! That is an idea! Are there others as handsome?

SALARET
Three at least—handsomer even.

RIFFONI
It would be a pity to leave them to Cazotti

SALARET
Damn him!

RIFFONI
Is it too late to collect them? . . . What glorious revels we could hold in the moonlight!

SALARET
Glorious! . . . Ah, you mean to kill me! Armida has betrayed me.

RIFFONI[*The pistol in his hand*]
You have betrayed the Republic—and with it humanity's last hope. We were to show ourselves supermen, you and I. A simple soldier, unscrupulous in his profession, puts us to shame as men even. Ah, I was ready to credit to nerves as tired as mine your despair of our work, to attribute your seduction of me to solicitude for my happiness. But I did not know you were a Tartuffe and a thief, that the Workers' Republic was to you merely a treasury and a brothel. Judas!

SALARET [*Stung by the exaggeration of this tirade to face his accuser, and finding himself desperately calm, now the long suspended sword has fallen*]

Ah, Vittorio, you make me wonder what is to be said for Judas? Men are not so simple. I sometimes think that monarchs who say "we" are the only true psychologists. How could I not care for the Republic —my whole life-work? How could I not care for you, my life-long supporter? Do you think I had no moments of heart-sickness when you turned the State my books projected into a shambles? I defended you before the Duke, but he was right. You would not wait to educate and evolve: your Socialism is only of the forcing house.

RIFFONI
But not of the bawdy-house.

SALARET
I know I fell. But if I tried to drag you down, too, my motive—believe me—was not wholly selfish, nor wholly without risk. Even more than Molp I was trembling for your safety.

RIFFONI
I was not playing for safety, but for achievement.

SALARET
You are sure it was not for power? You speak as if I alone had sucked voluptuous profit from the Republic. Your lust of blood wrought infinitely more misery than my lust of the flesh.

275

RIFFONI
My lust of blood?

SALARET
Even now you are yielding to its secret lure.
   [RIFFONI *lowers his pistol*]
Shall I ever forget how you gloated over the asphyxia-
tion of Prince Igmor? You must be in at the death,
you said. Was it because Igmor dared to love your
darling? And then your lust for applause. Never
to move without salvos from reeking guns and stinking
lungs.

RIFFONI [*Overwhelmed*]
If you knew how I have longed to be a shepherd in his
wicker-work hut, open to wind and weather!

SALARET [*Sarcastically*]
And in practice you make a throne-room your bureau
and a throne your office-chair — do not tell me you
sleep on a camp-bed, it is the same megalomania, aping
a Napoleon on his campaigns. And this passion of
yours that I sincerely sought to gratify, even if it
gratified my own, why was it for Margherita and no
lesser woman? Cazotti was right—the thought of
fondling a Queen tickled you, as Napoleon with titil-
lated by an Emperor's daughter.

RIFFONI
Have done! Travesty me if you will, but not my
thought of Margherita. Is it not enough she has
276

faded into the inaccessible—like all my visions of the Republic? . . . Ah, to what end do all these mirages beguile our souls? Why are we not as the animals, which have ignorances but never illusions?

SALARET
And why hug the illusions, since not being animals we can grow in wisdom? Kill me if you will, Vittorio— I have had such hours as I did not even know life held, when I was merely a scribbling phantast, a biped with a quill. He who shoots at a star misses. Let us proportion our aim to our reach. Can you learn nothing from life?

RIFFONI
I am too tired—I can learn only from death.
    [HE *mounts the stone step before the plain case-ment and throws it open. The light has been fad-ing and the snow mountains appear, rosy with sunset. A few stars are already twinkling*]
Why is the mob grown silent?

SALARET
The guillotine was all but up when I came by—the thought of death must be awing them.

RIFFONI
What children! It is life that is awesome, not death. . . . Ah, there she goes, the yacht, like youth throb-bing with purpose? And there rolls the purposeless universe, drifting like an old hulk in the ocean of space. . . . On this very balcony, Salaret, my father died, in his dream of love. And my forcing house is

277

as visionary.   Ah, they are both futile, force and love,
while our breed remains so poor.
   [*Steps out.*]
Where are you going?

RIFFONI
To my father!
   [*Disappears on the balcony.   A shot rings out.*]

FENELLA'S VOICE [*Yelling from below*]
Riffoni is dead!   *Viva* Cazotti!

CROWD [*In Piazza, echoing her*]
Cazotti!   Cazotti!   *Viva* Cazotti!
   [OMAR *rushes in.*]

SALARET [*Gazing out*]
You are spared a crime.   He is dead.

OMAR
You have killed him?

SALARET
Yes, God help me.
   [HE *falls on the stone step.   The cheers for*
   CAZOTTI *swell into a great rolling thunder.*   OMAR
   rushes out through the pillars.   SALARET *graps*
   frenziedly at the Red Flag and tears it down]
The Republic is dead!   Long live King Cazotti!

CURTAIN.

By
ISRAEL ZANGWILL

The War God
Plaster Saints
Chosen People
Ghetto Comedies
Ghetto Tragedies
Italian Fantasies
The Melting Pot
The Next Religion
Jinny, The Carrier
The Voice of Jerusalem
The King of Schnorrers
Children of the Ghetto
The World and the Jew
The War for the World
The Principle of Nationalities
The Cockpit

THE FORCING HOUSE

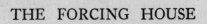